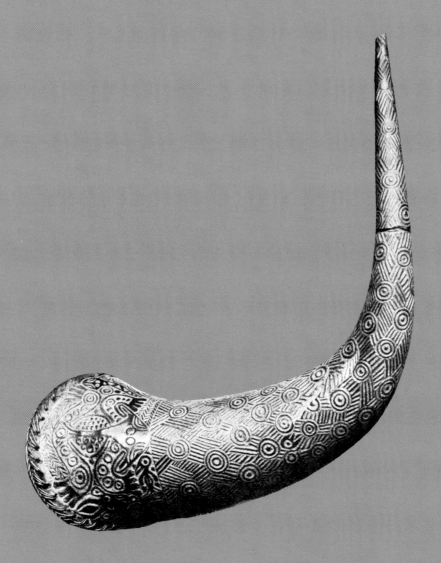

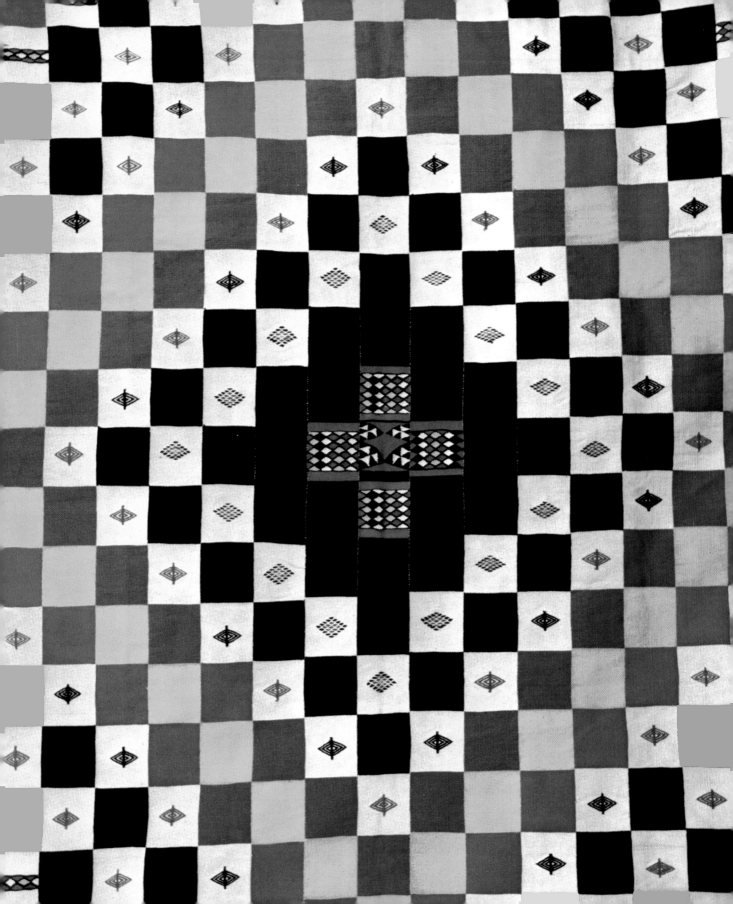

AFRICAN DESIGN

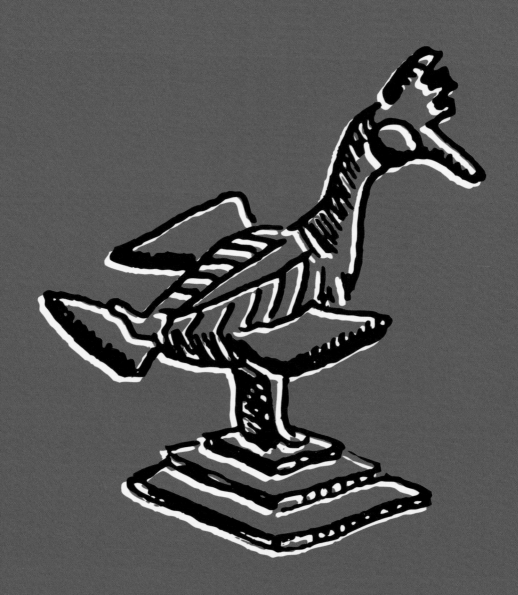

AFRICAN DESIGN

DOVERPICTURA

DOVER PUBLICATIONS, INC. | Mineola, New York

Selected and designed by Luisa Gloria, Joel Waldrep and Alan Weller.

African Design is a new work, first published by Dover Publications, Inc.,
in 2007.

The CD-ROM file names correspond to the images in the book. All of the artwork
stored on the CD-ROM can be imported directly into a wide range of design and
word-processing programs on either Windows or Macintosh platforms. No further
installation is necessary.

ISBN 10: 0-486-99846-0
ISBN 13: 978-0-486-99846-6
Manufactured in the United States of America
Dover Publications, Inc., 31 East 2nd Street, Mineola, NY 11501
www.doverpublications.com

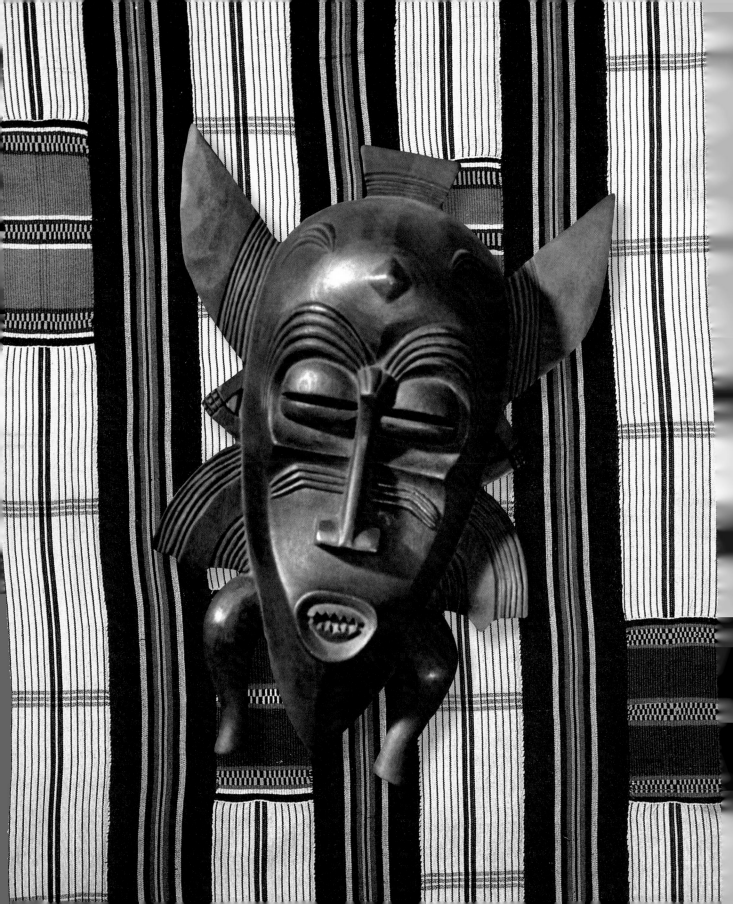

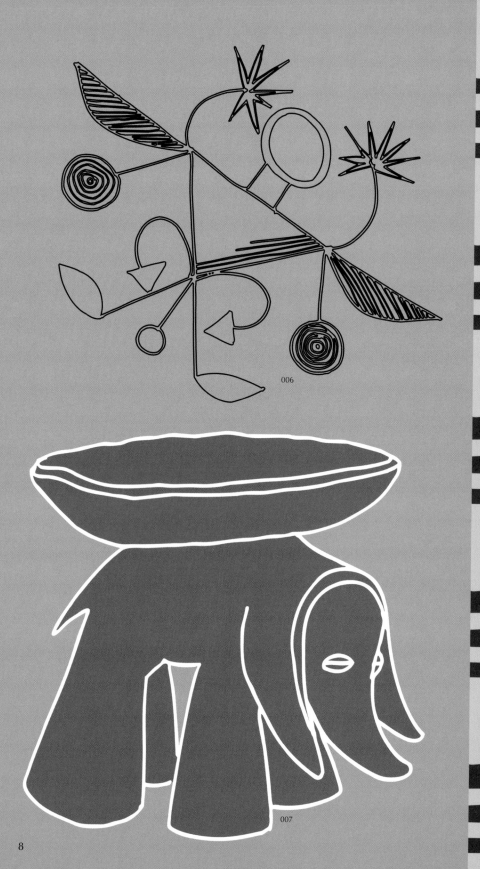

006

007

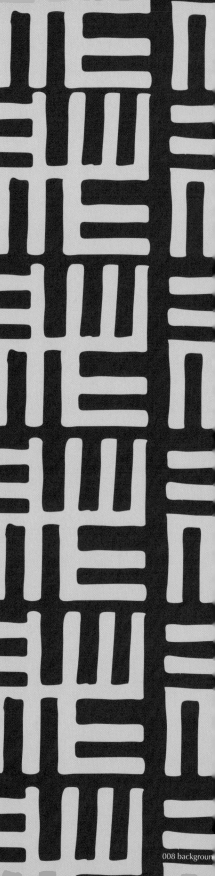

008 background

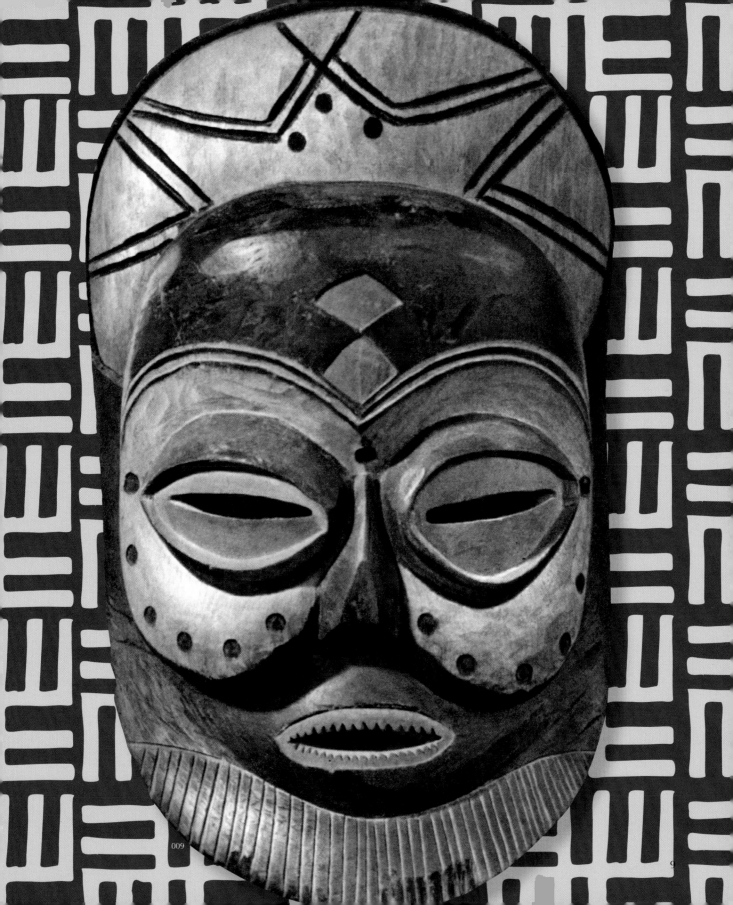

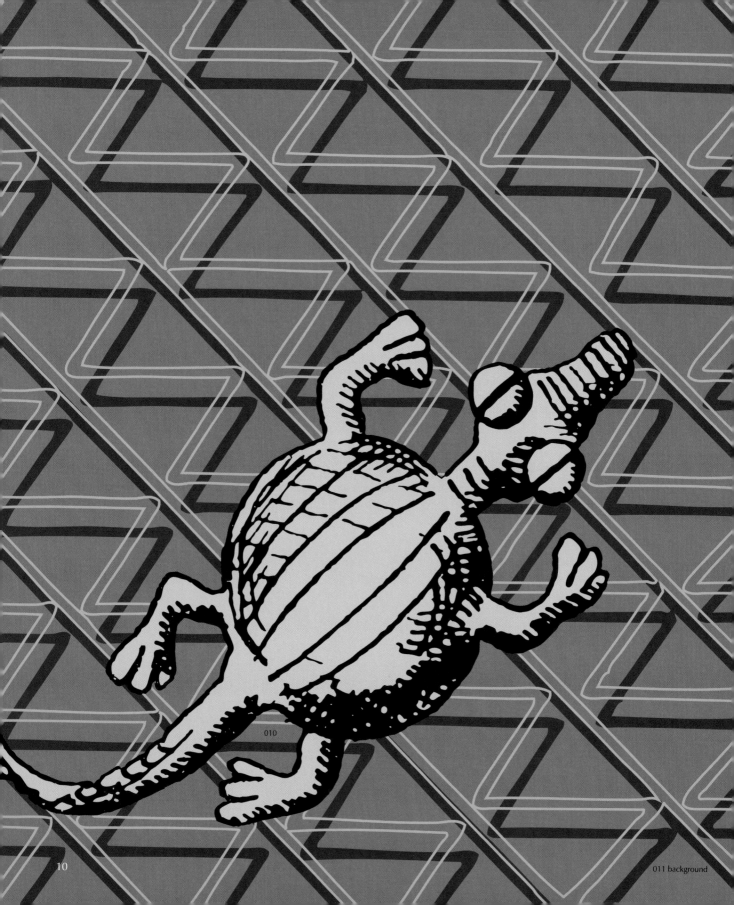

010

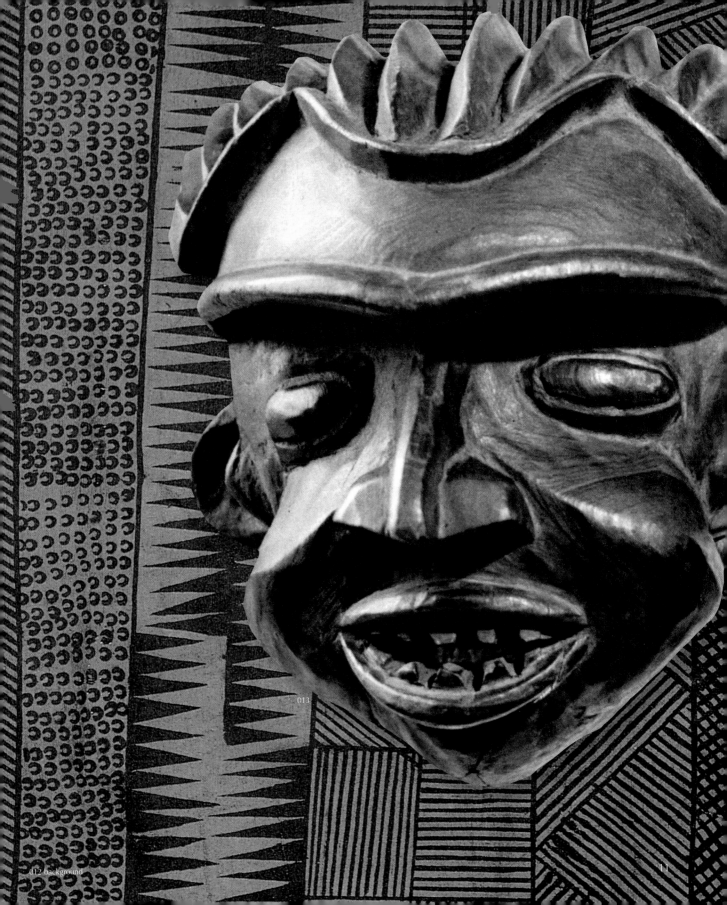

013

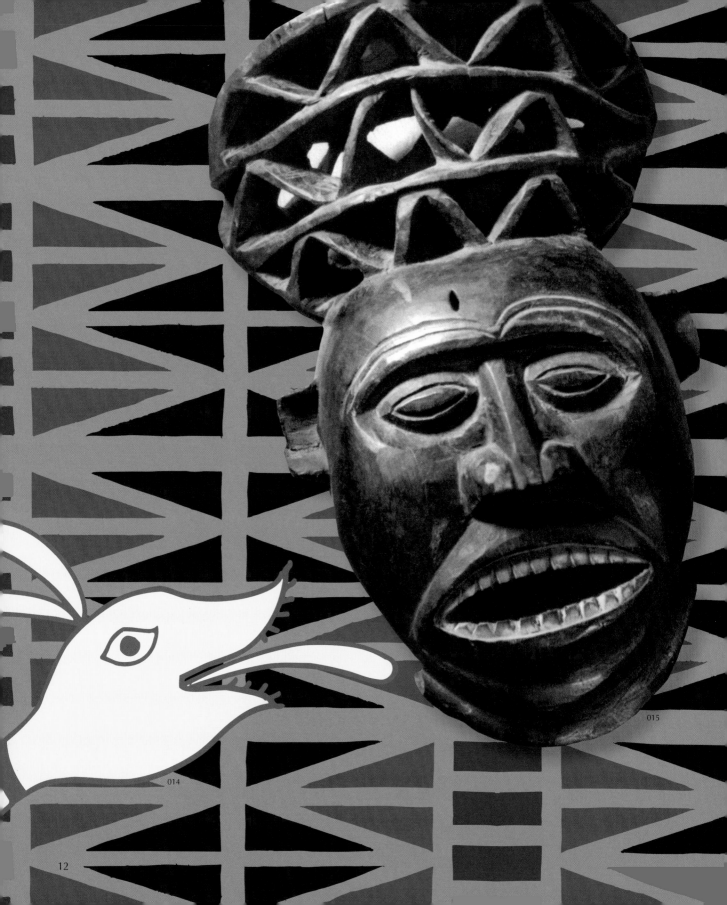

014

015

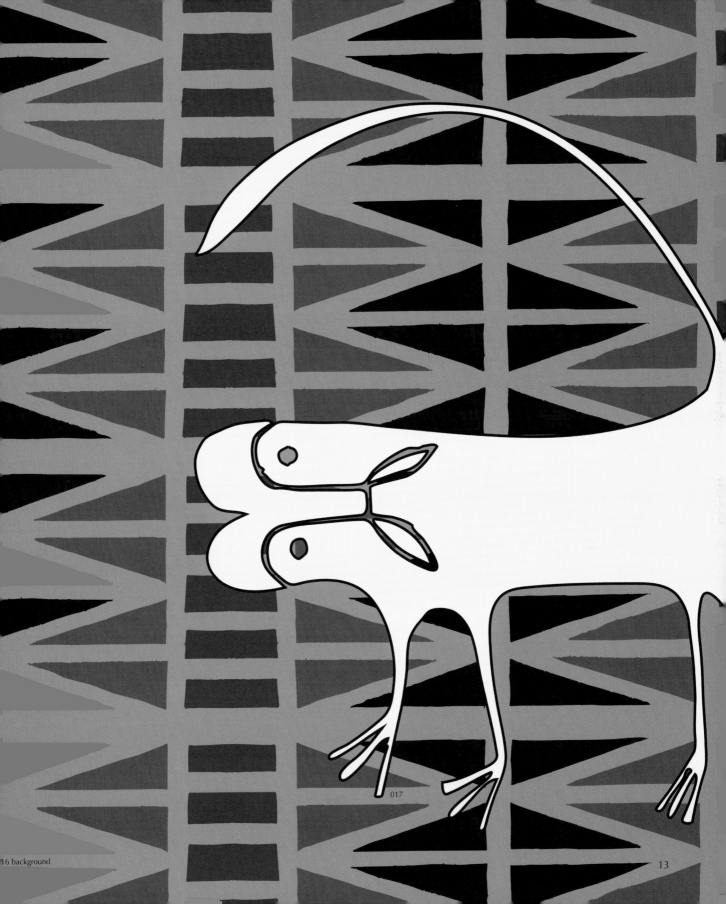

017

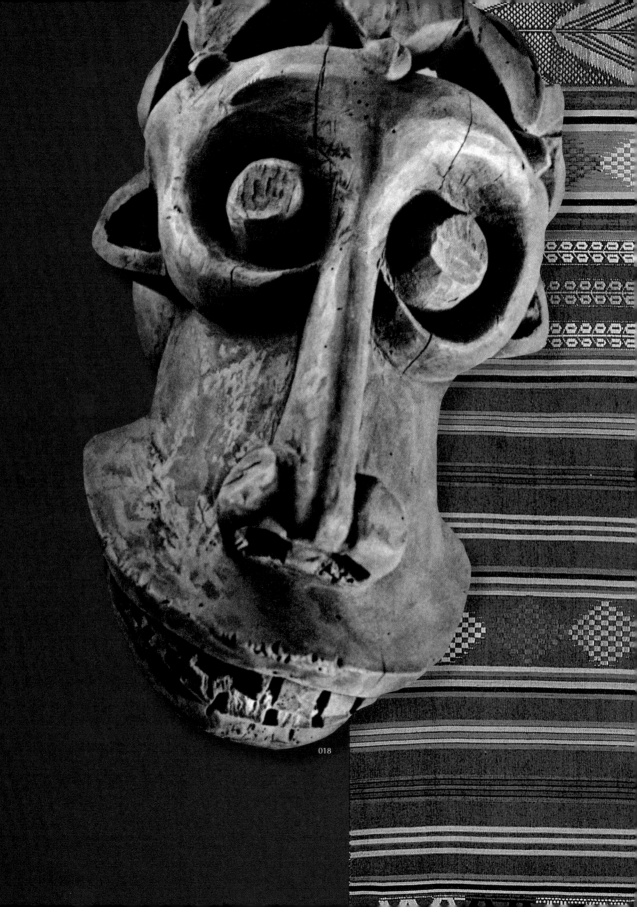

018

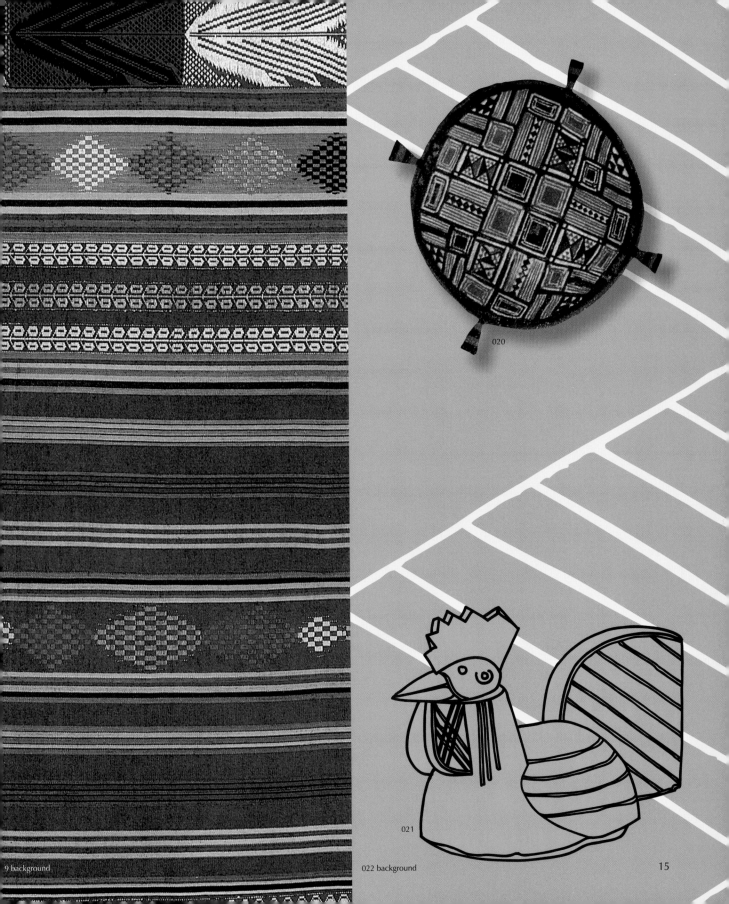

020

021

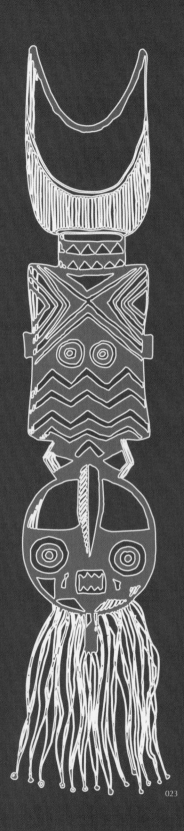

023

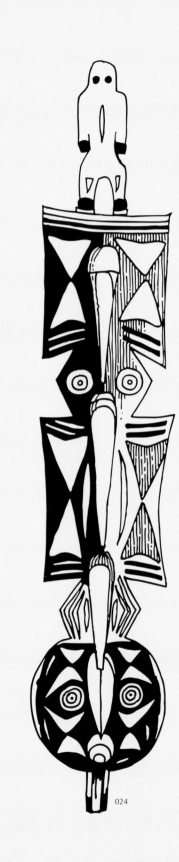

024

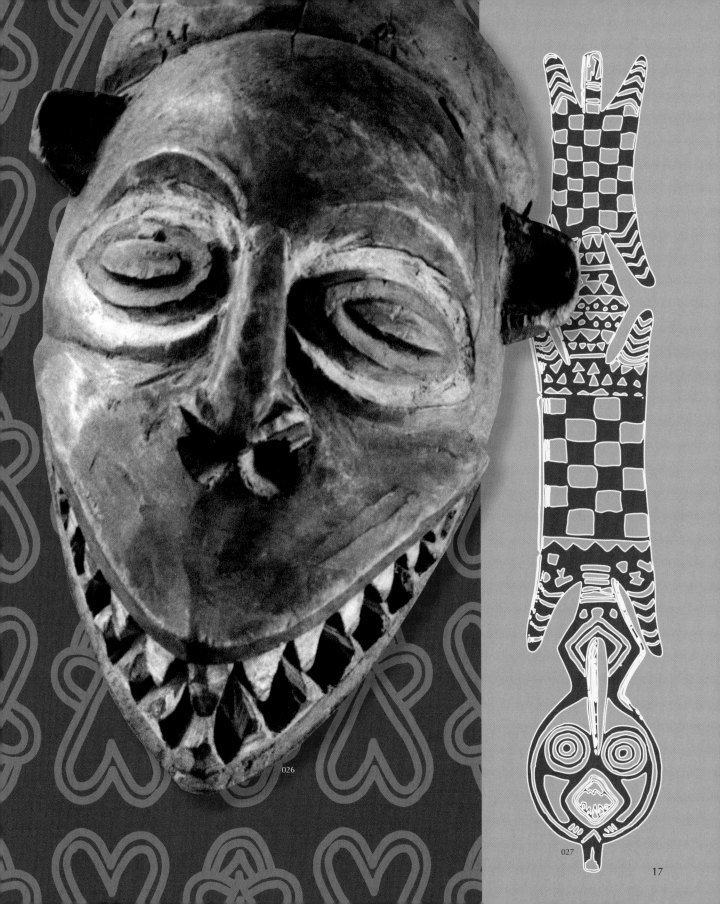

026

027

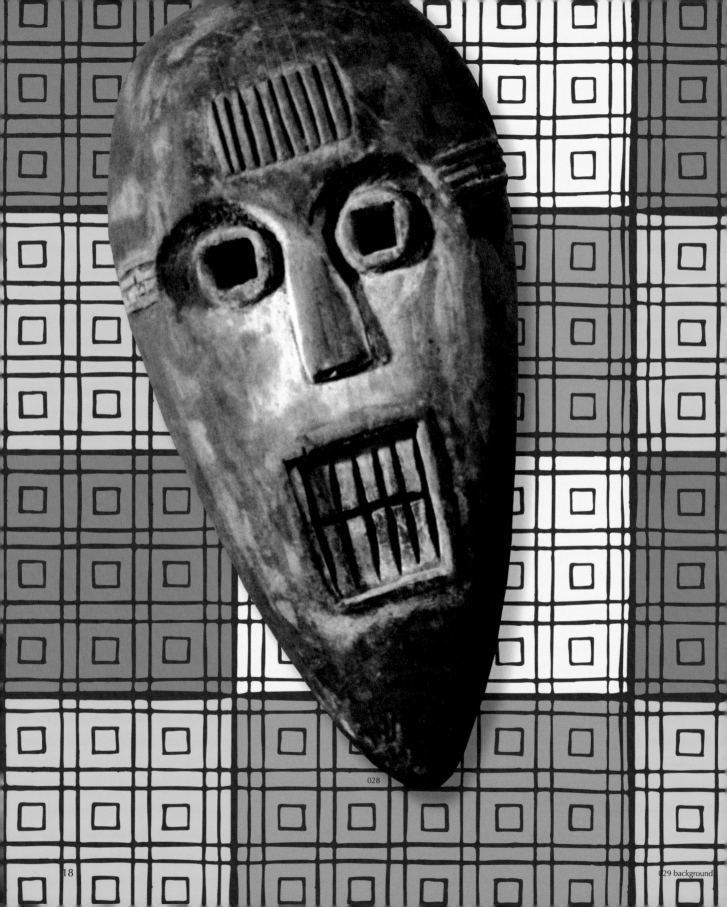

028

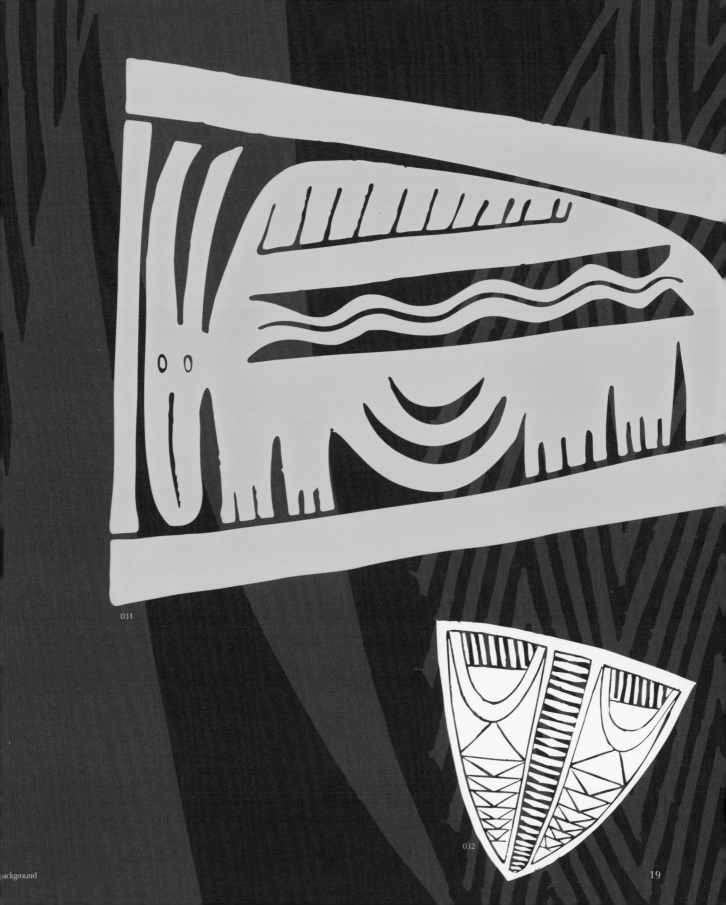

031

032

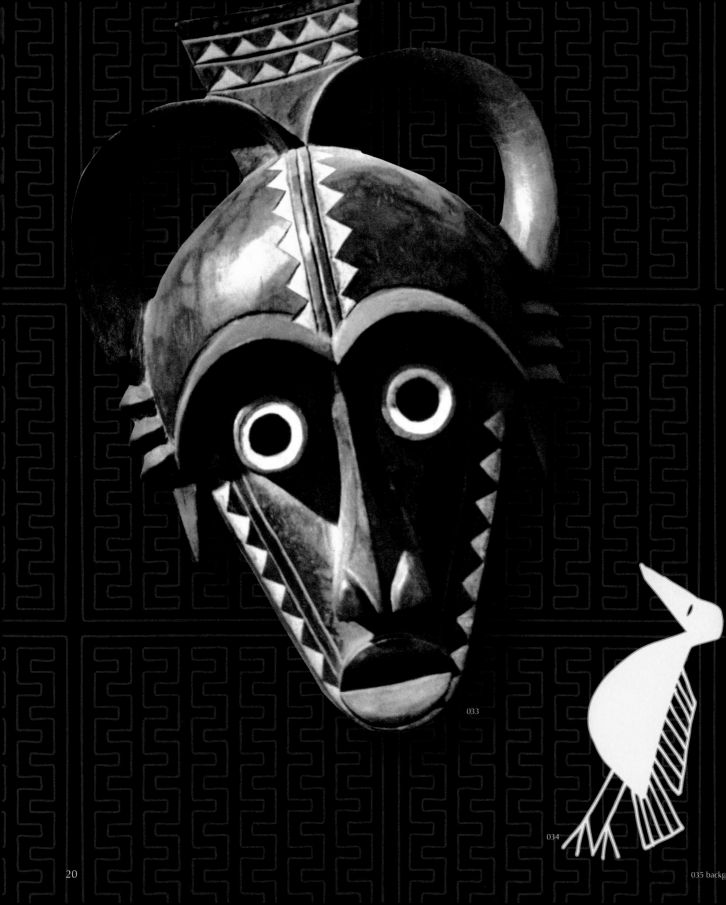

033

034

035 back

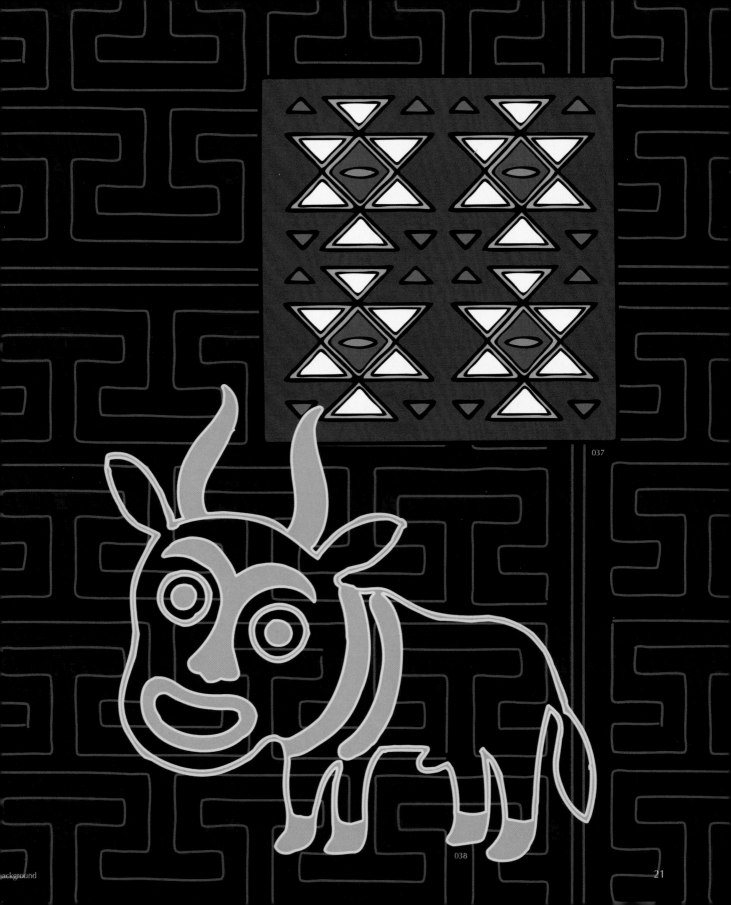

038

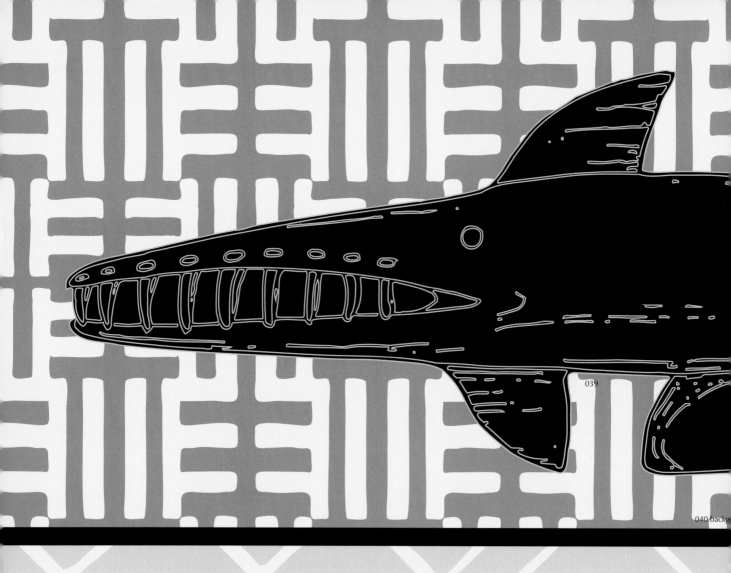

039

040/backg

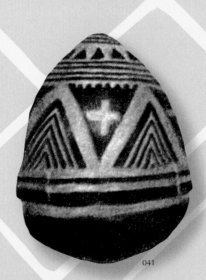

041

042 backg

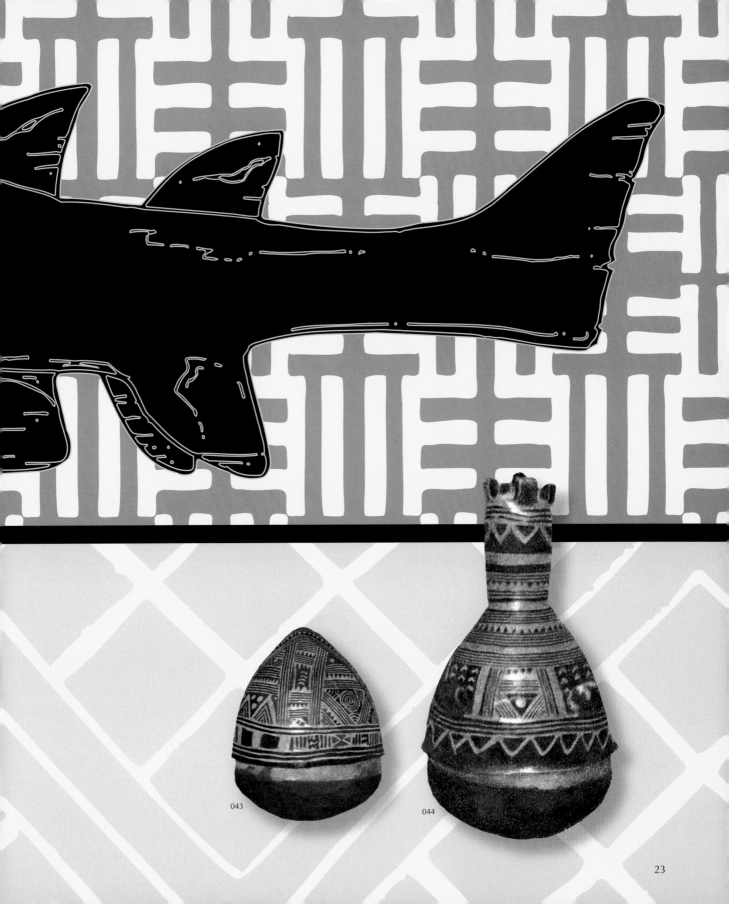

043

044

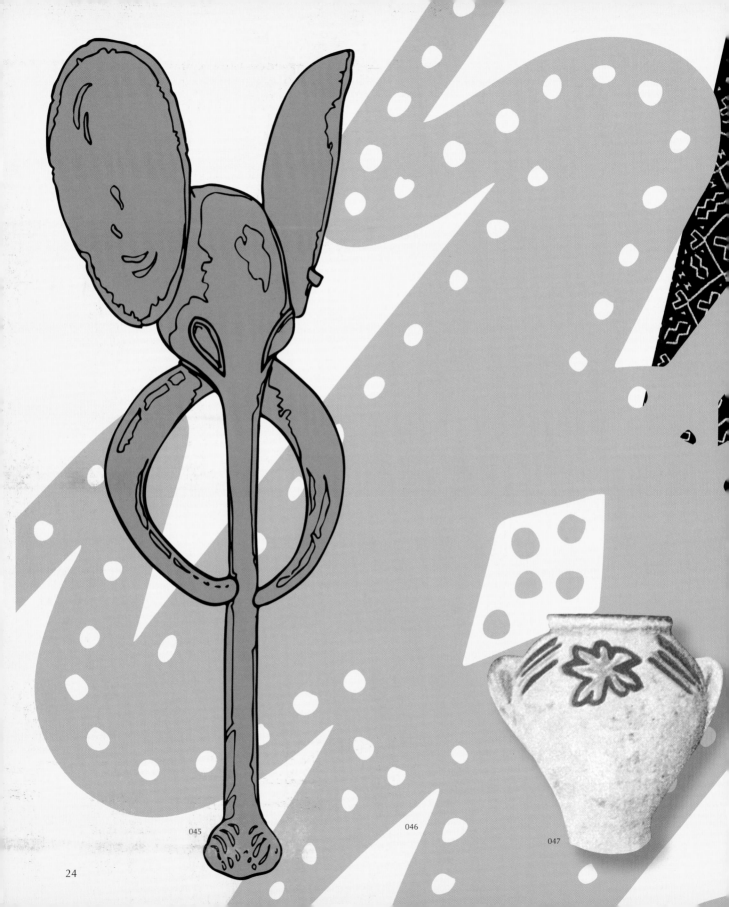

045

046

047

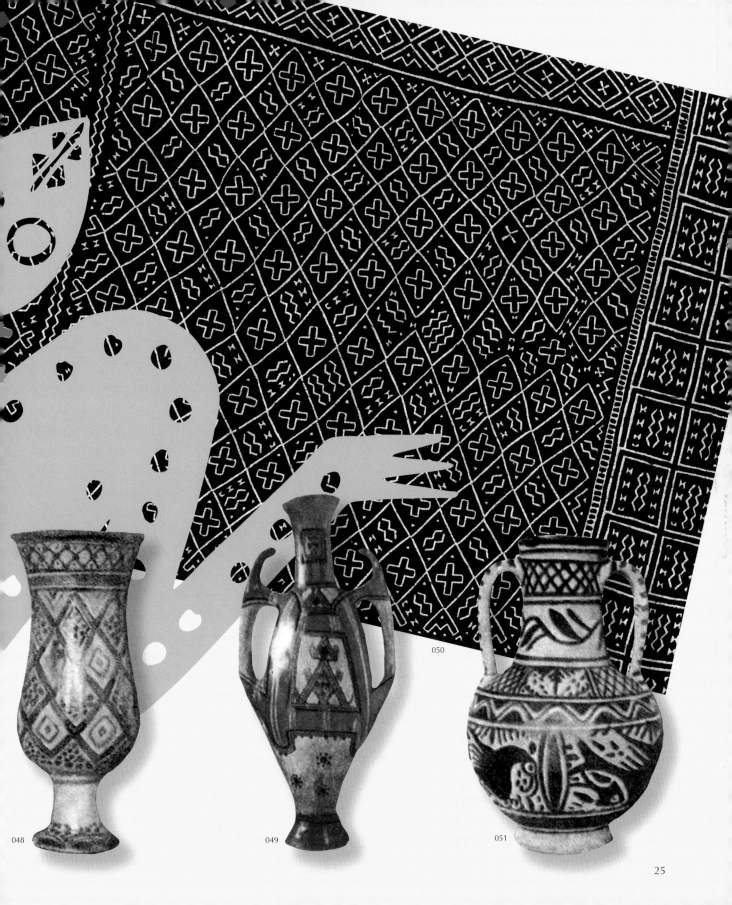

048

049

050

051

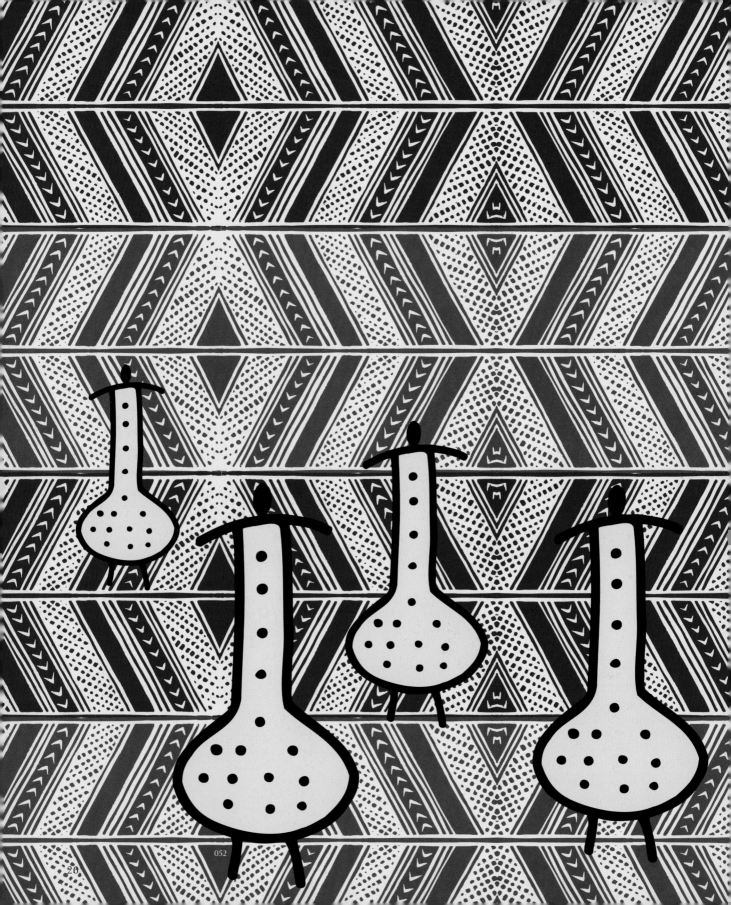

26

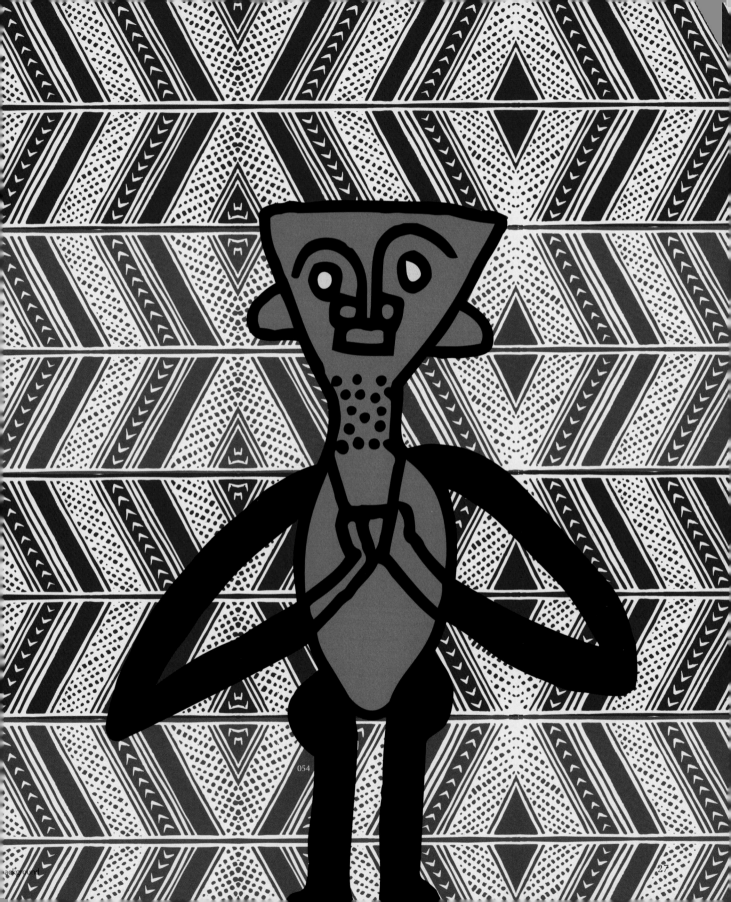

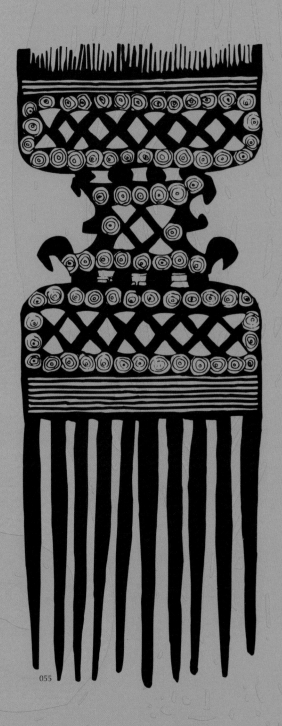

055

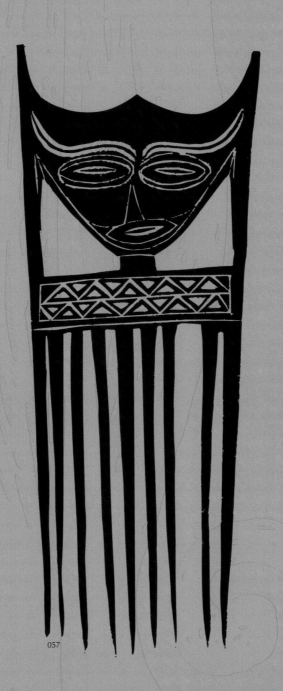

057

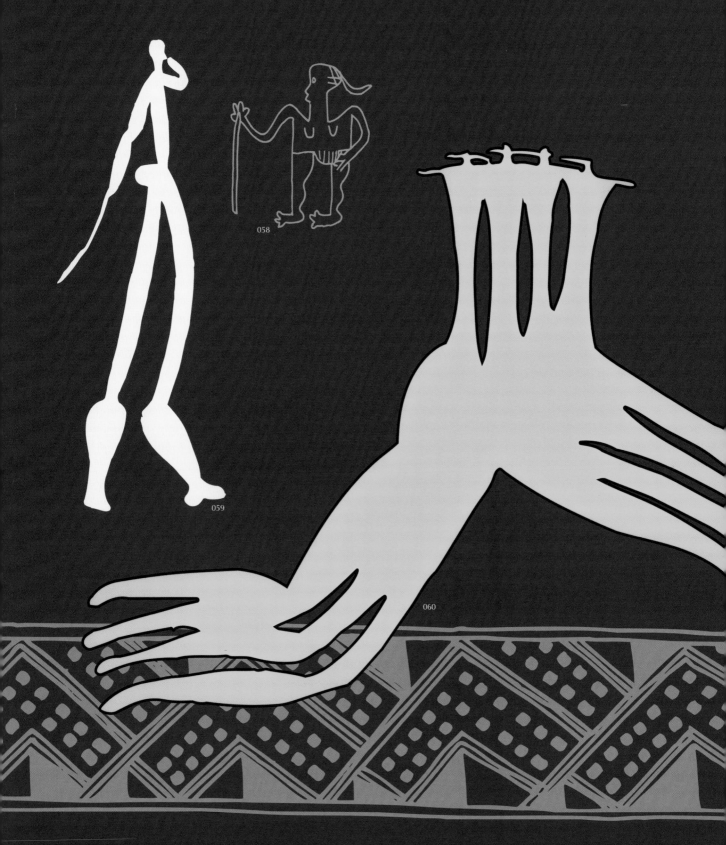

058

059

060

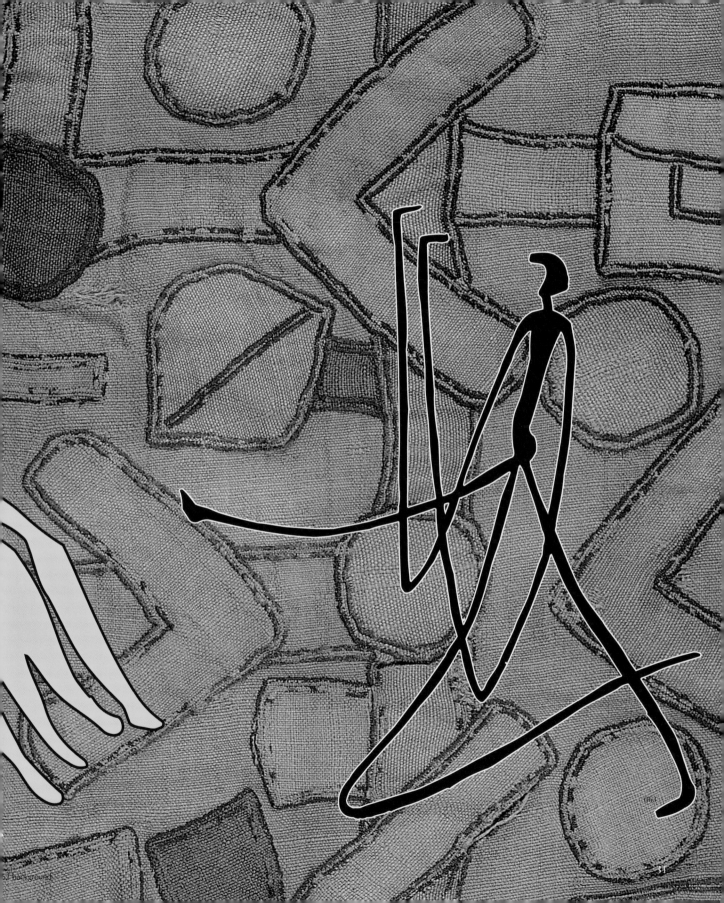

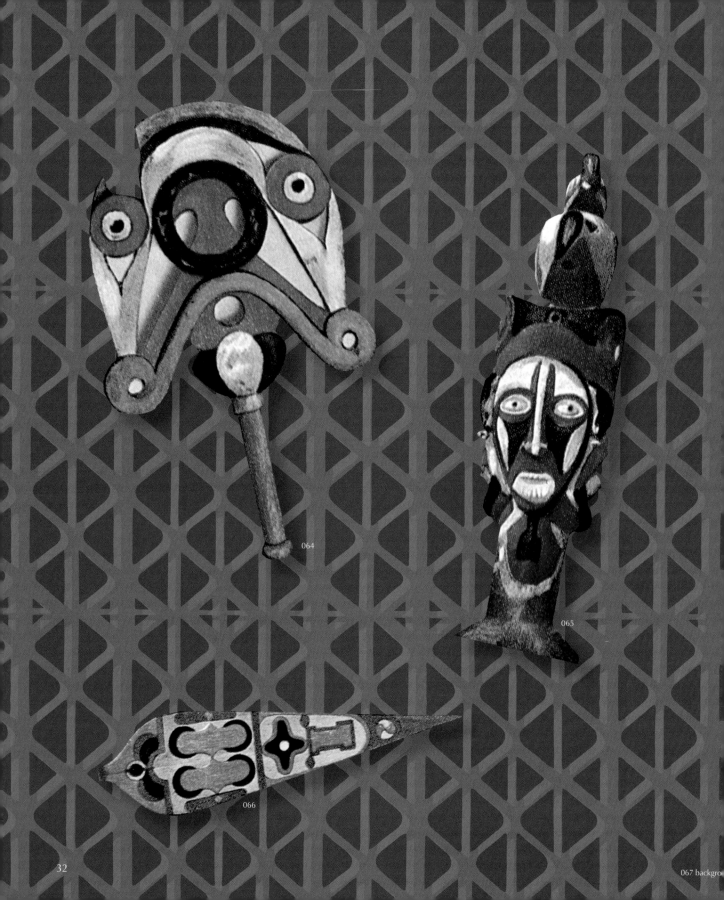

064

065

066

067 backgrou

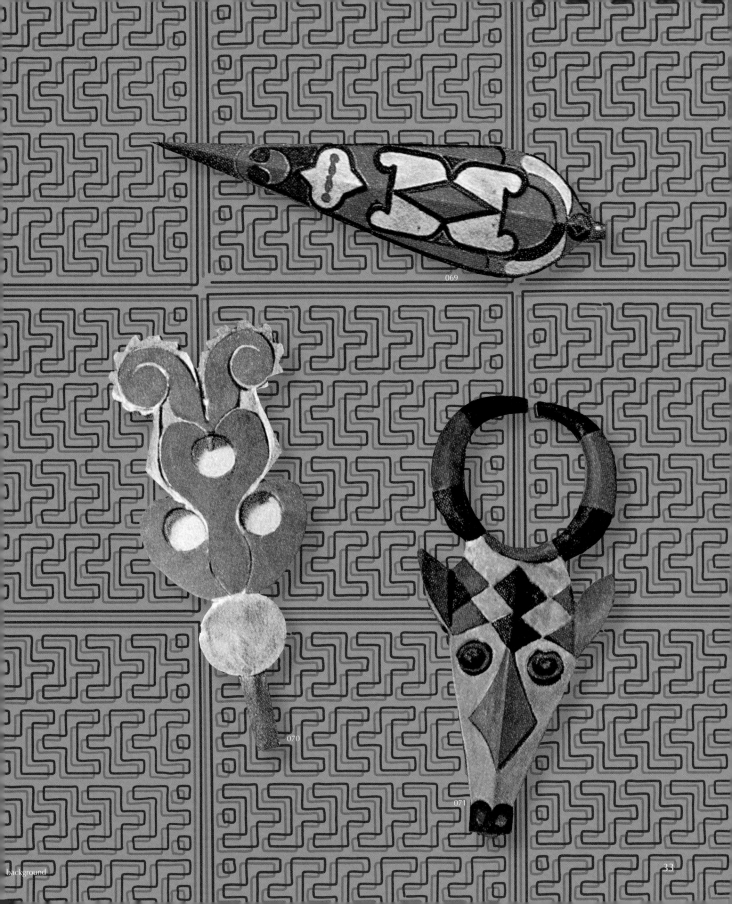

069

070

071

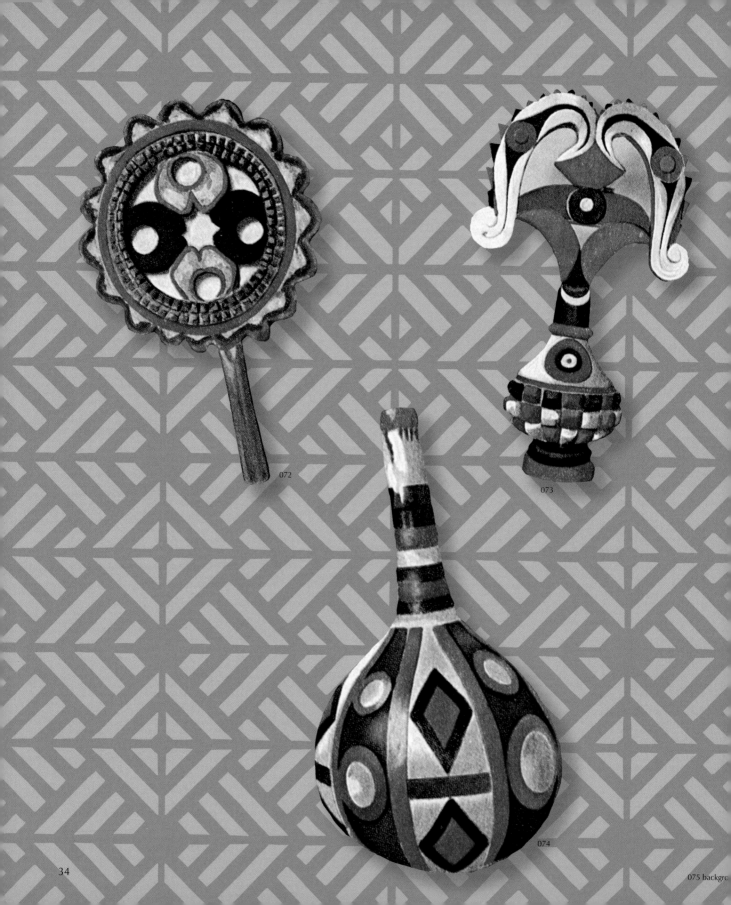

072

073

074

075 backgrᴏ

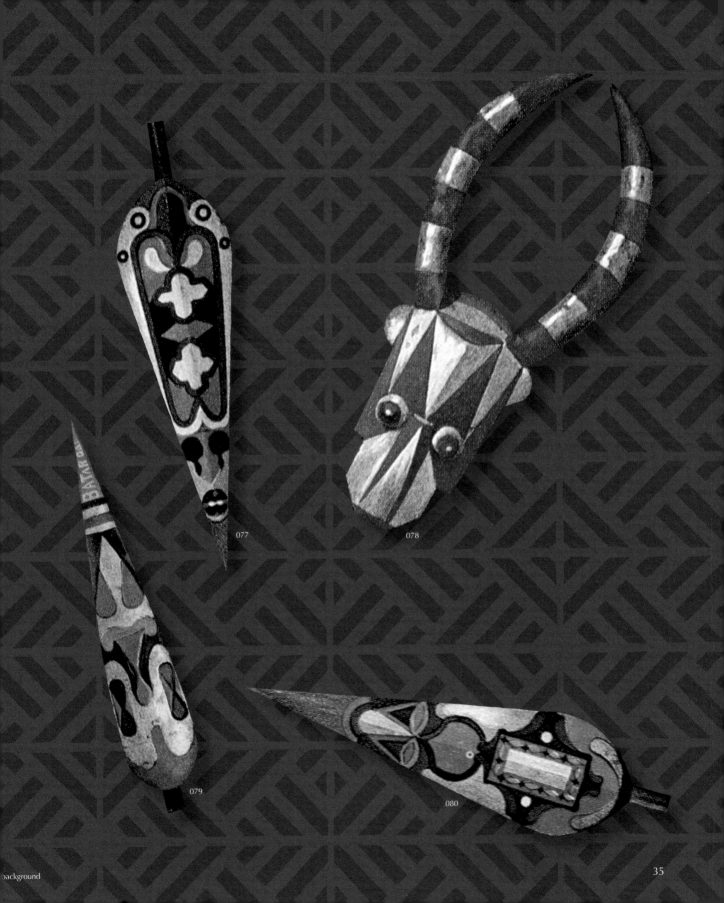

077

078

079

080

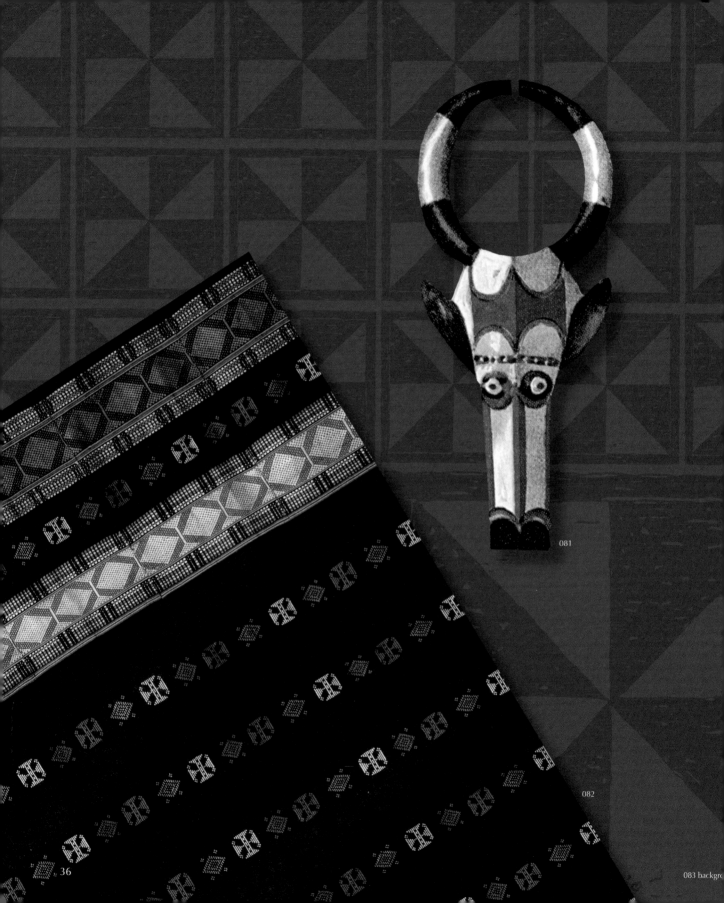

081

082

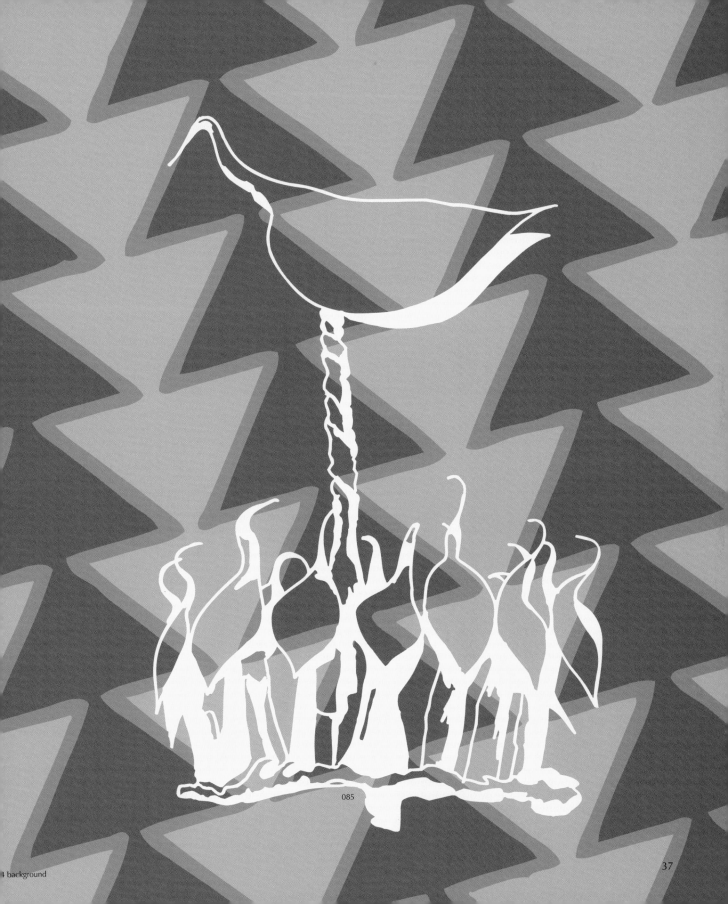

085

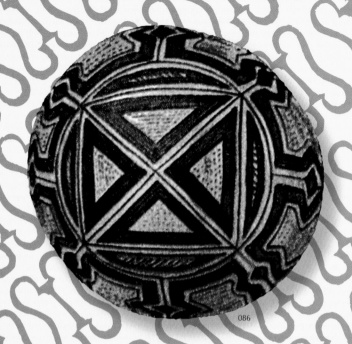

086

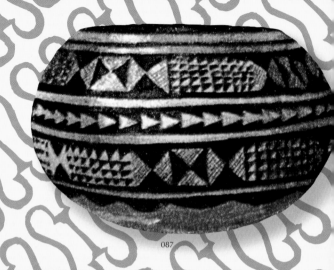

087

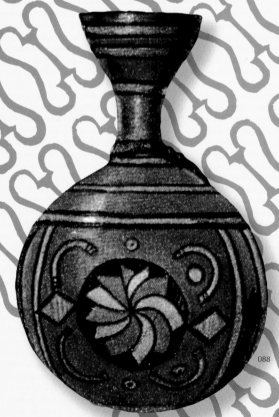

088

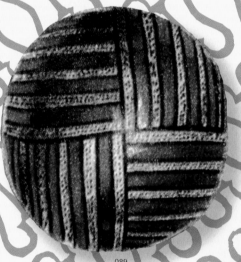

089

38

090 backgro

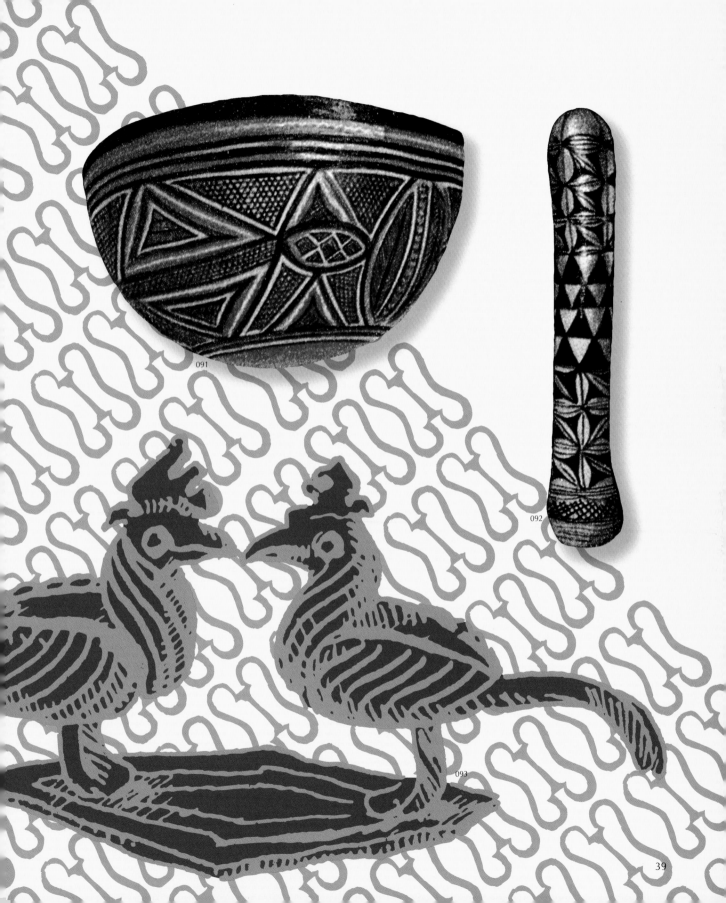

091

092

093

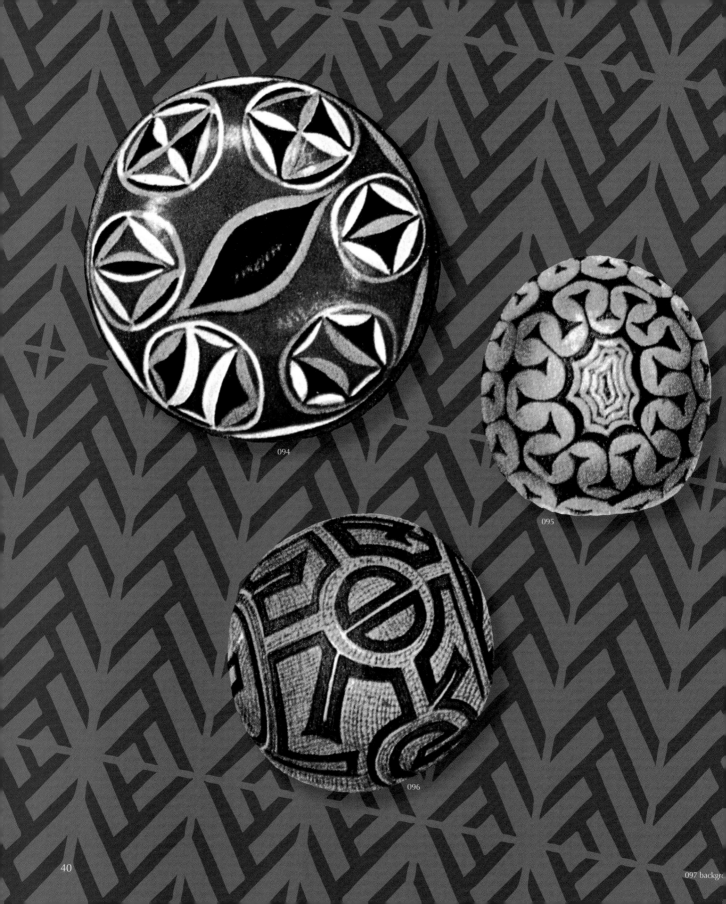

094

095

096

097 backgr

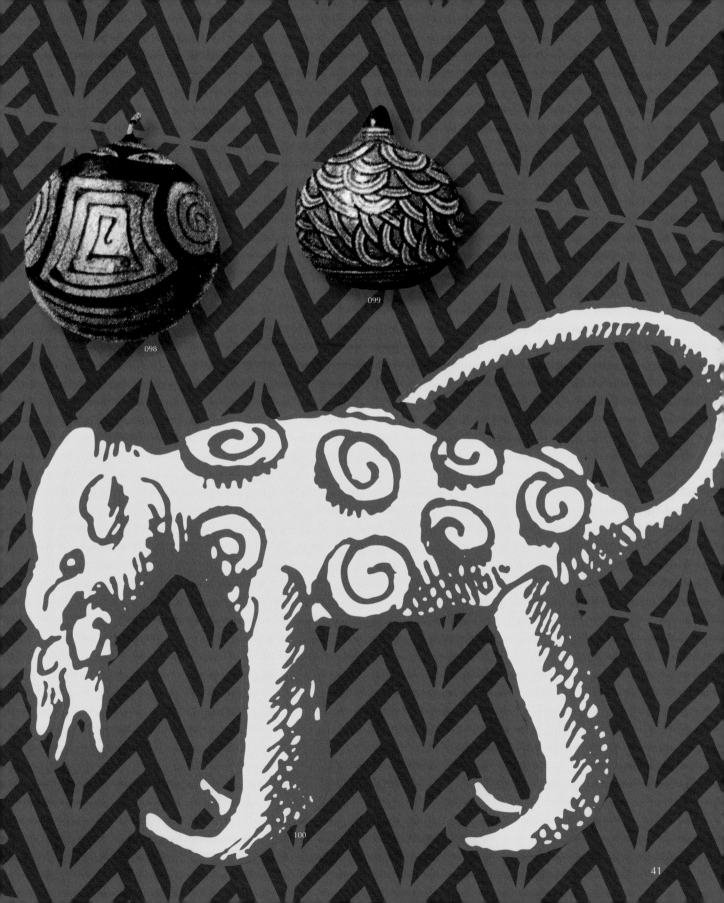

098

099

100

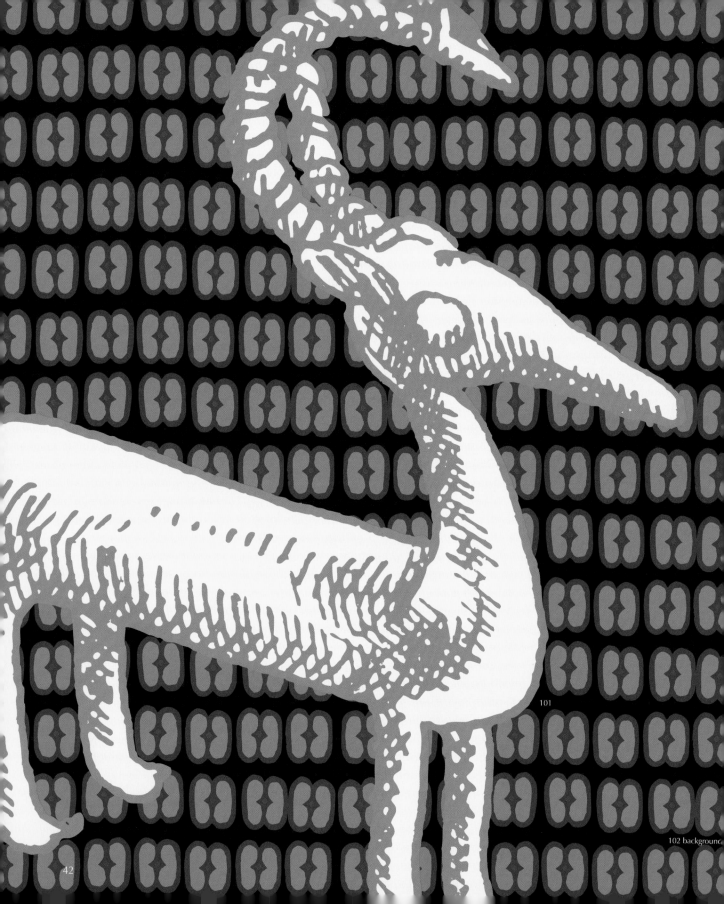

101

102 background

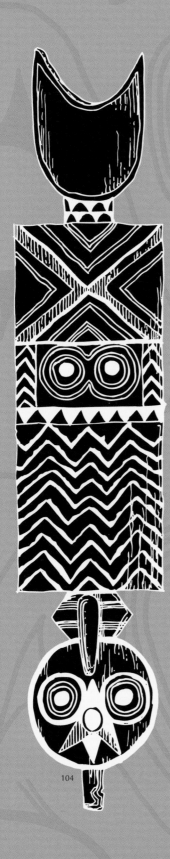

104

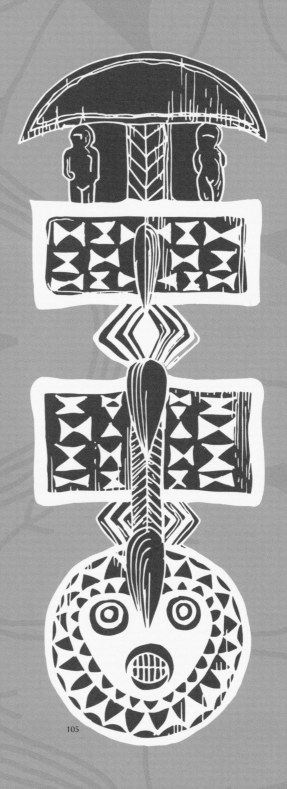

105

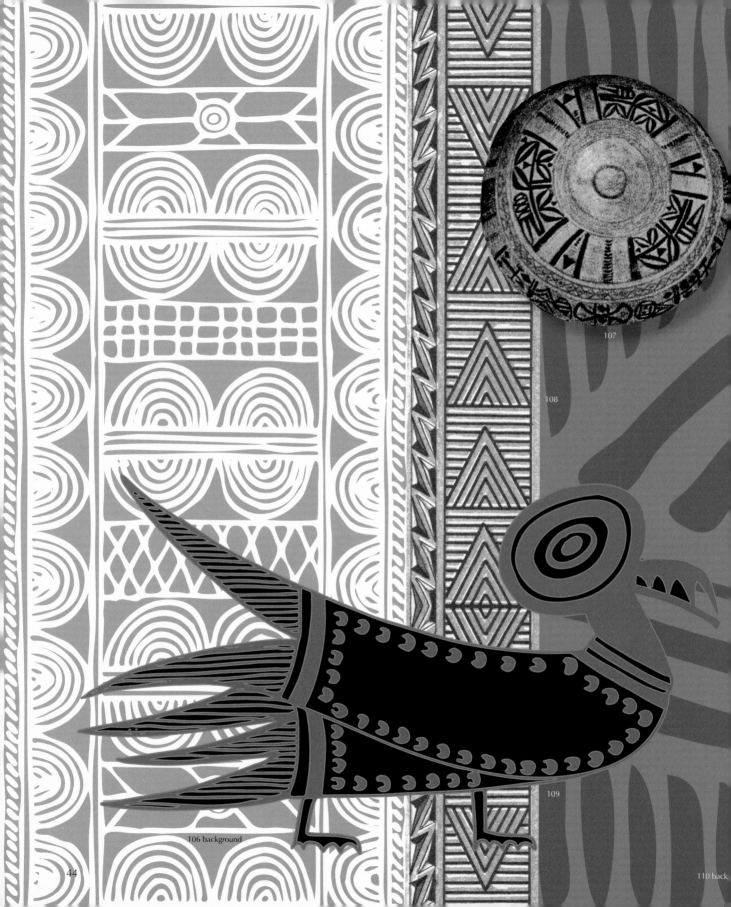

106 background

107

108

109

44

110 back

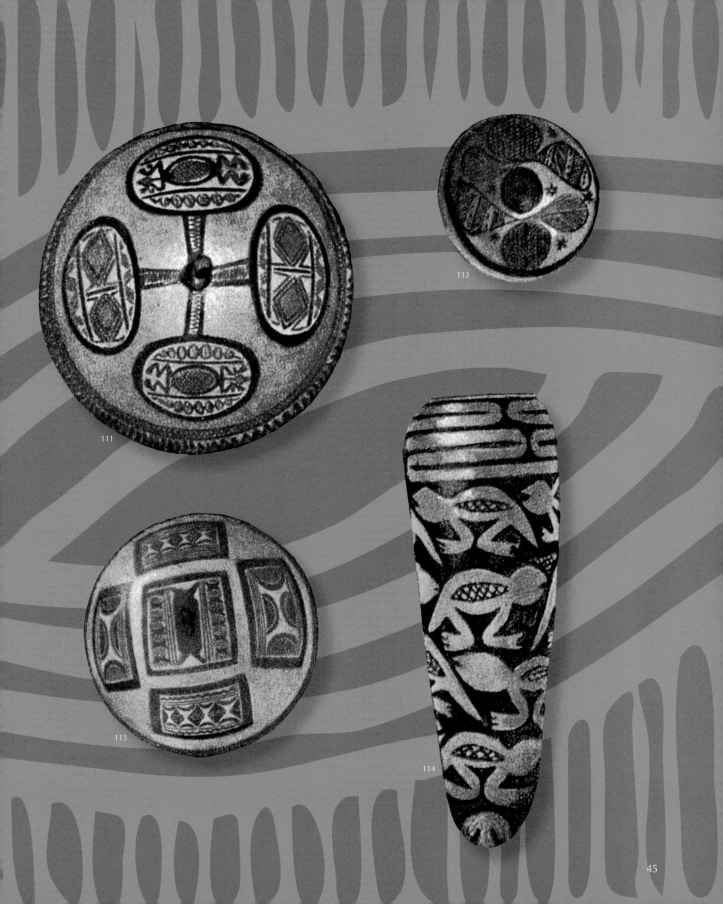

111

112

113

114

45

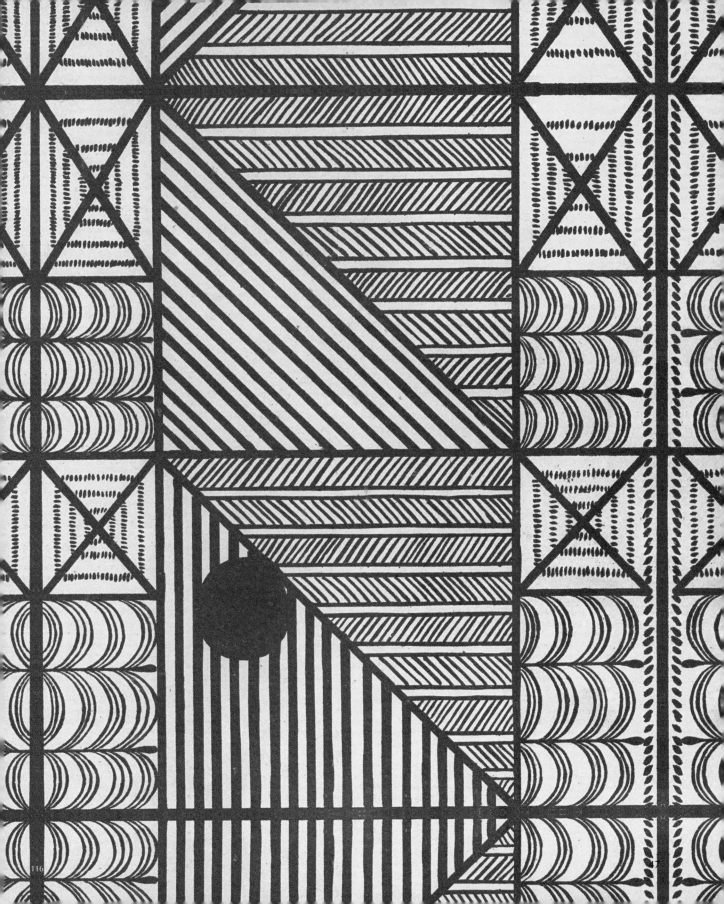

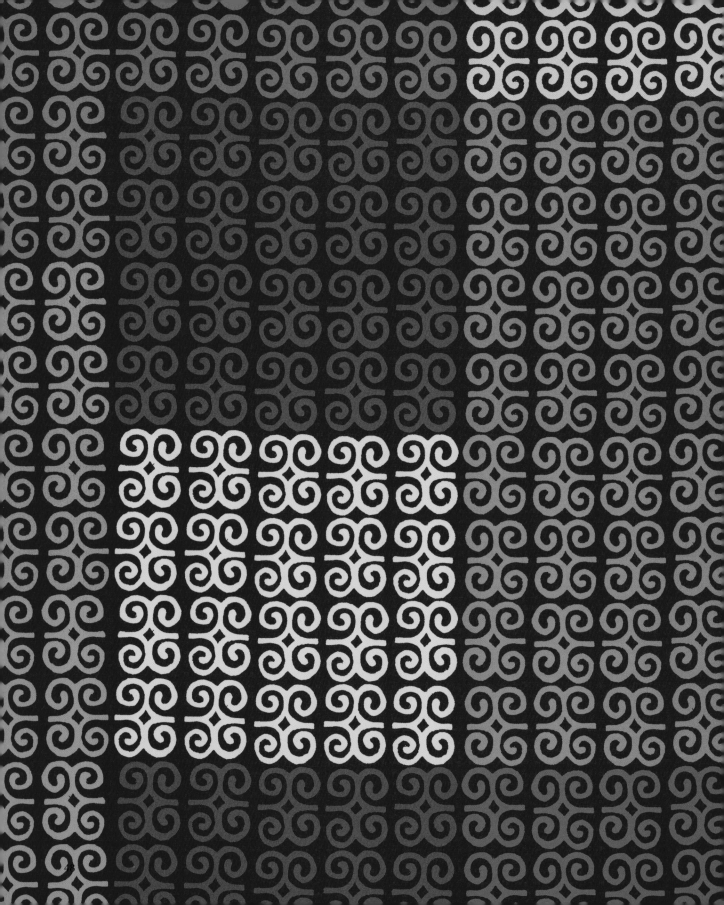

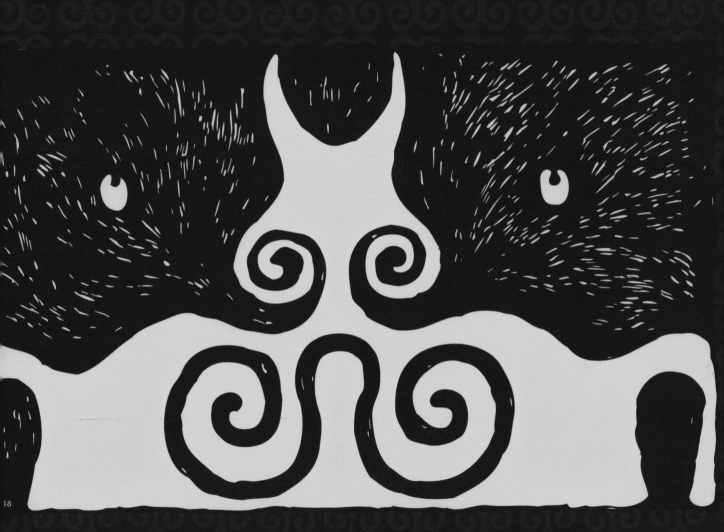

18

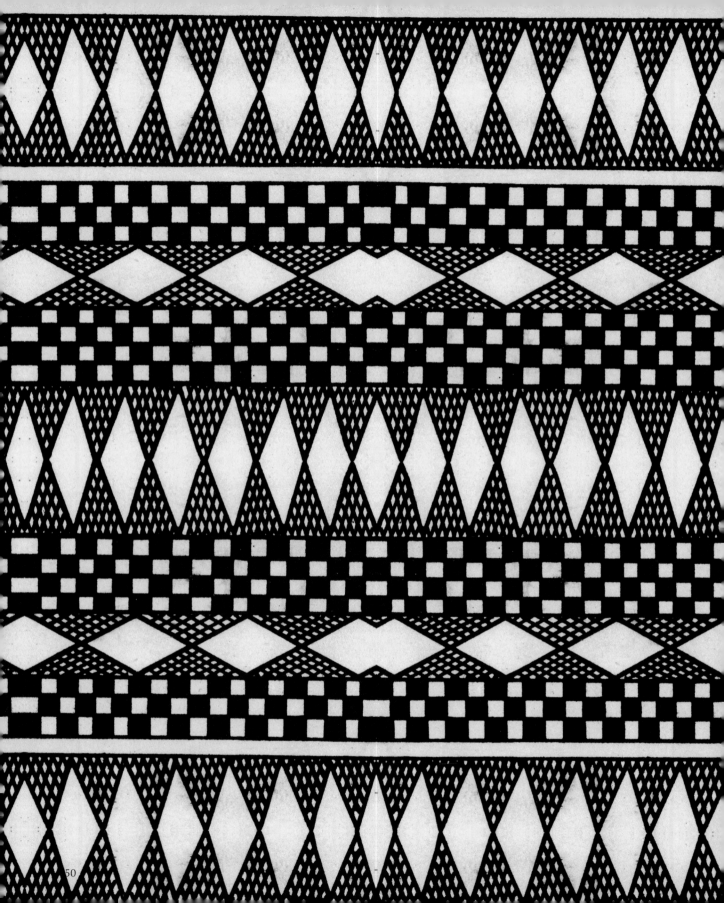

50

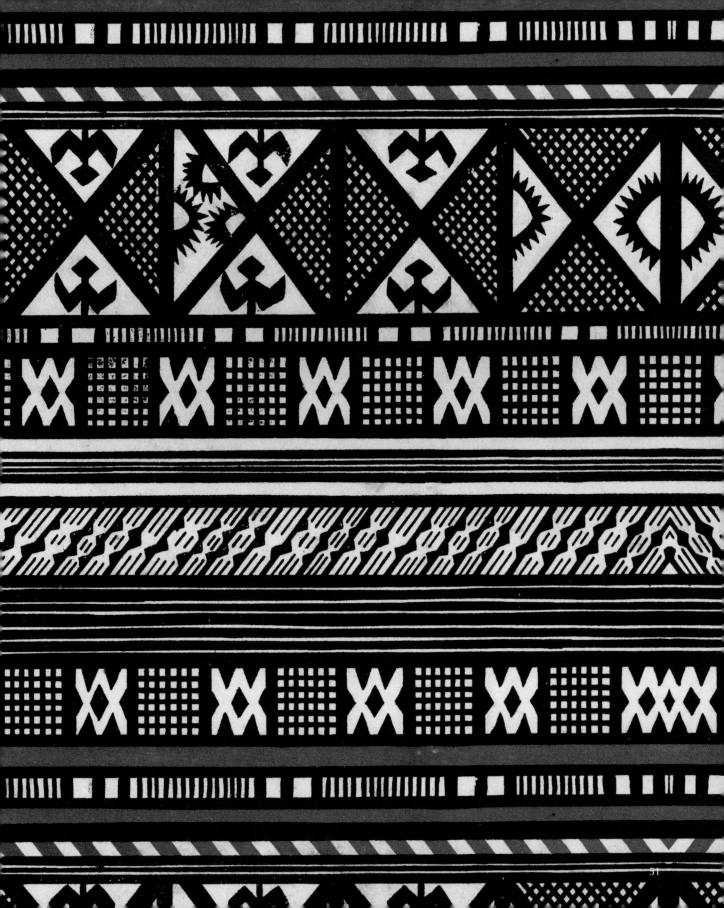

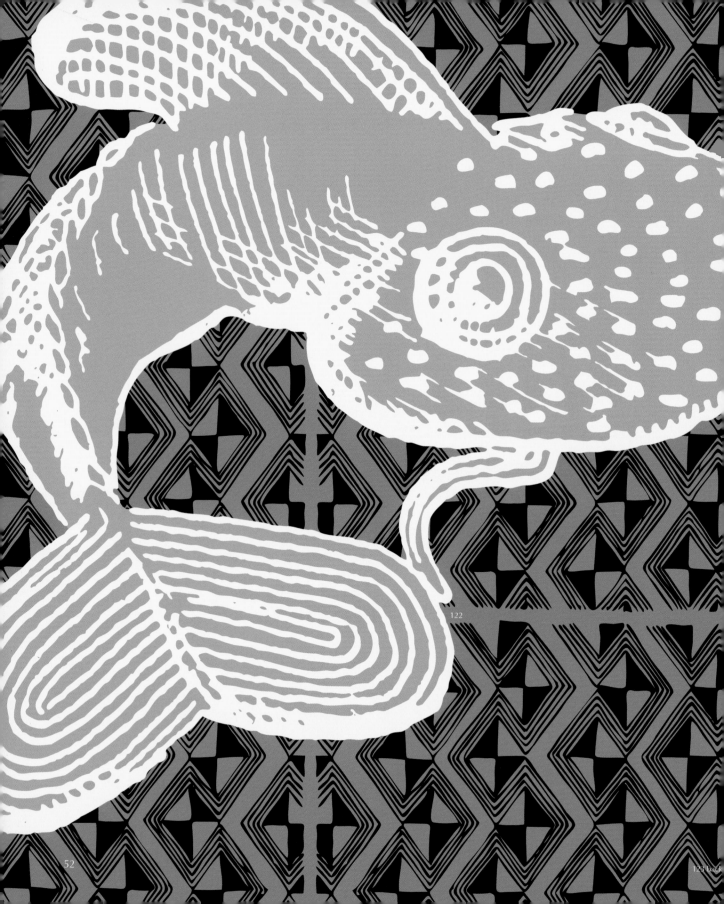

122

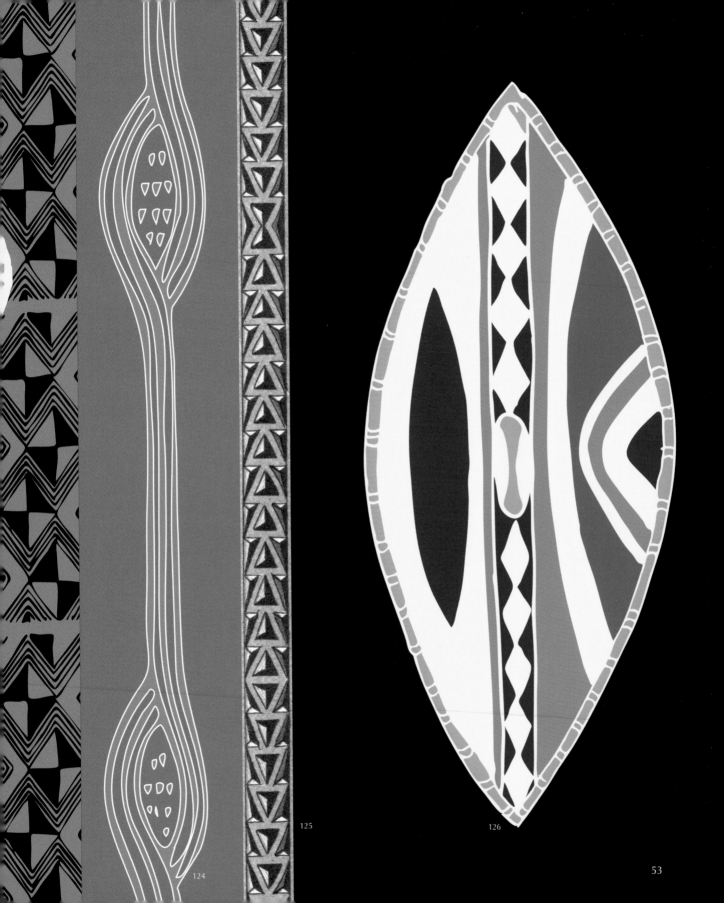

124

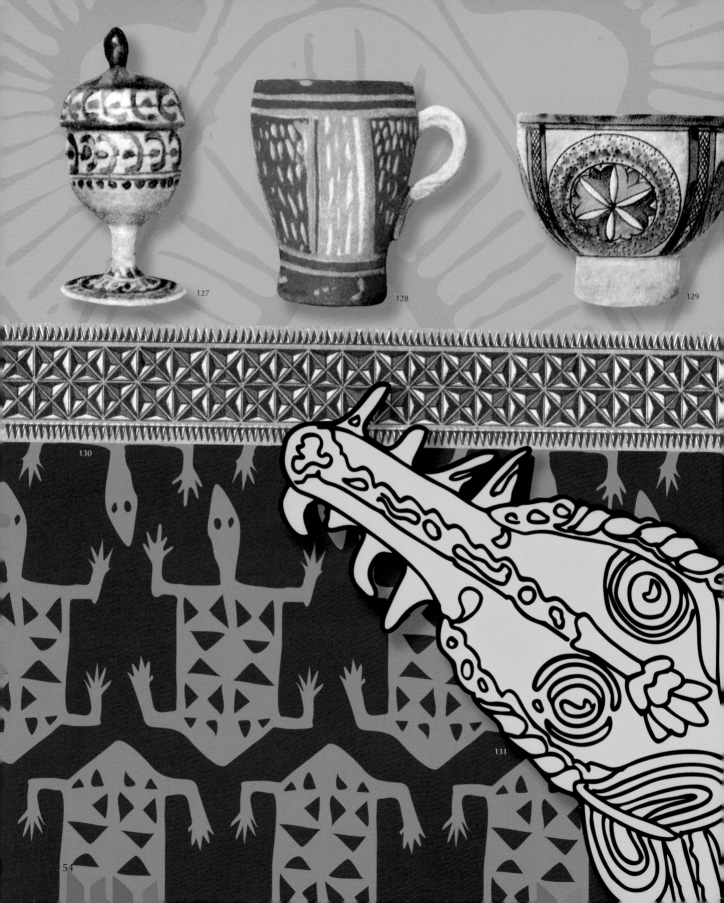

127

128

129

130

131

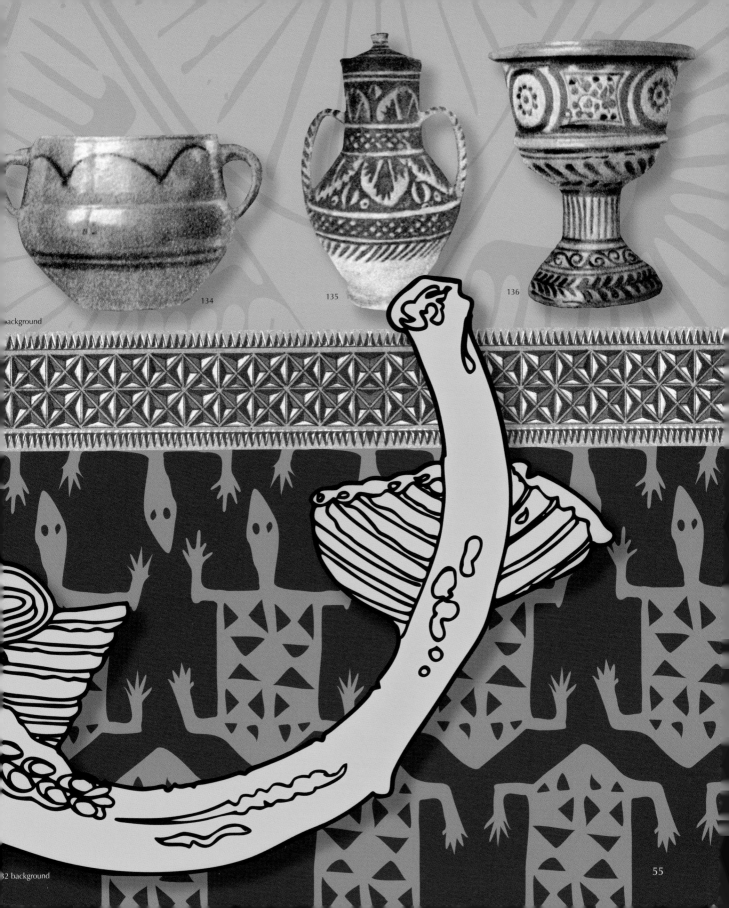

134

135

136

55

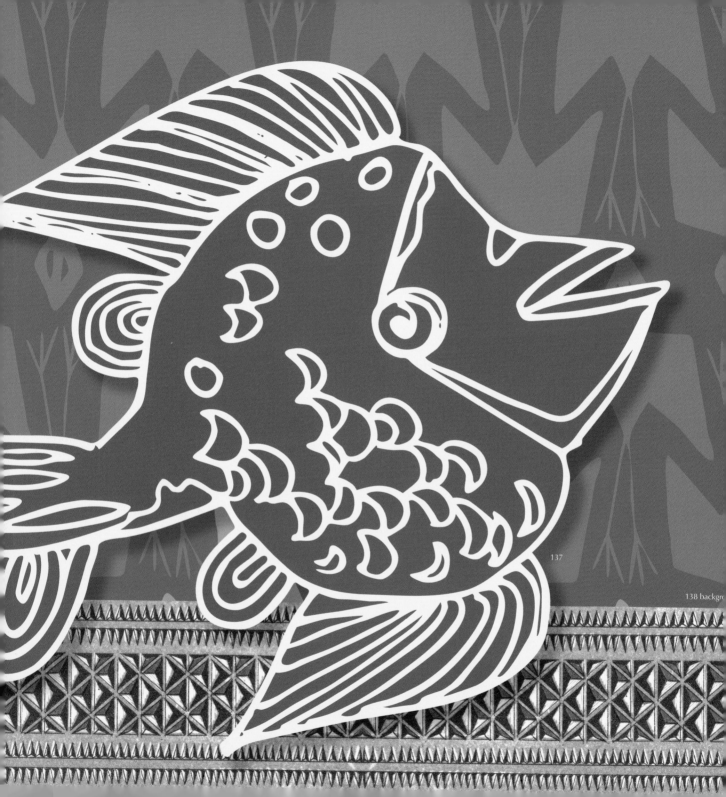

138 backgr

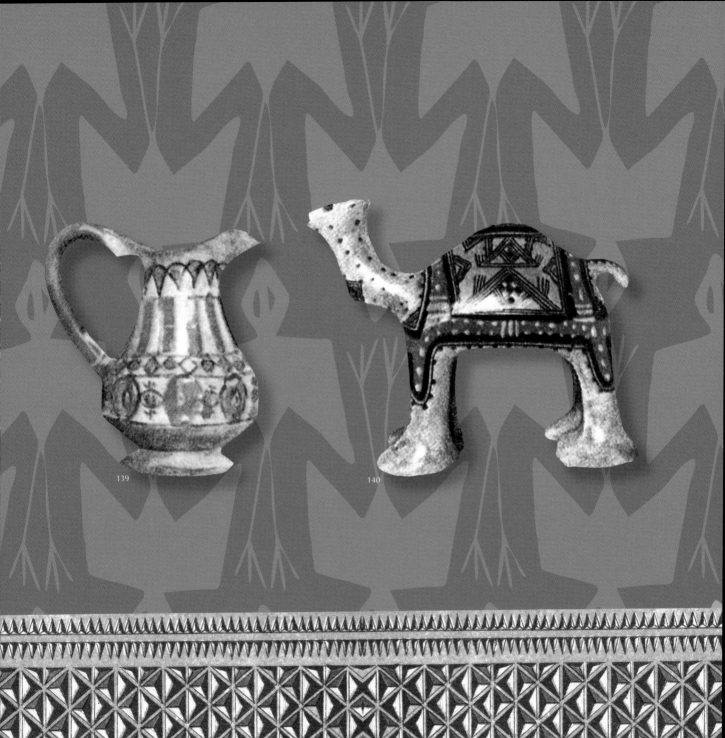

139

140

141

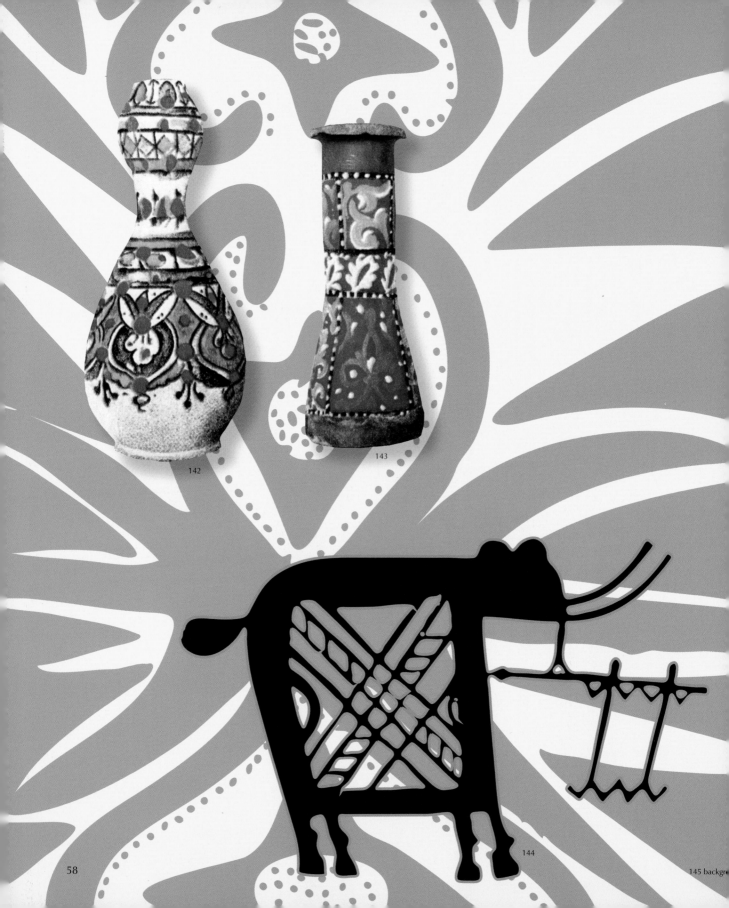

142

143

144

145 backgr

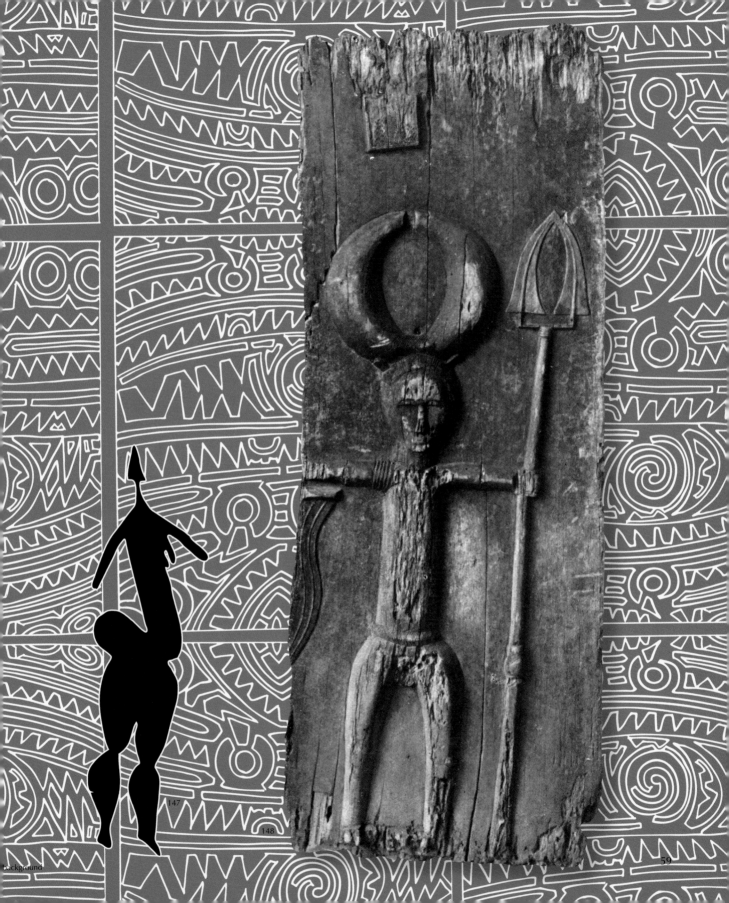

147

148

background   59

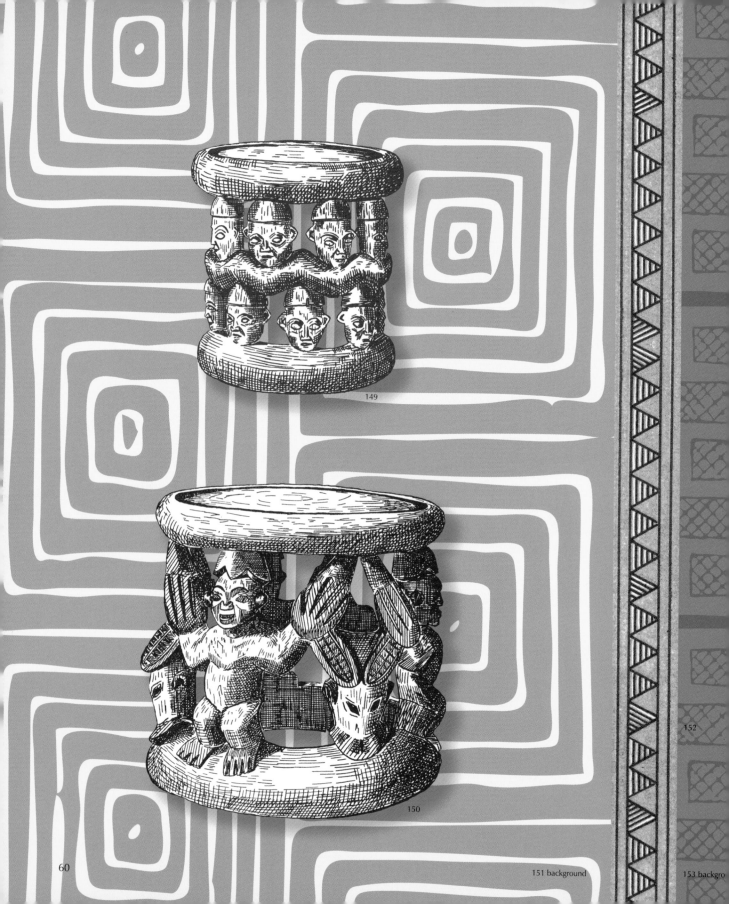

149

150

151 background

152

153 backgro

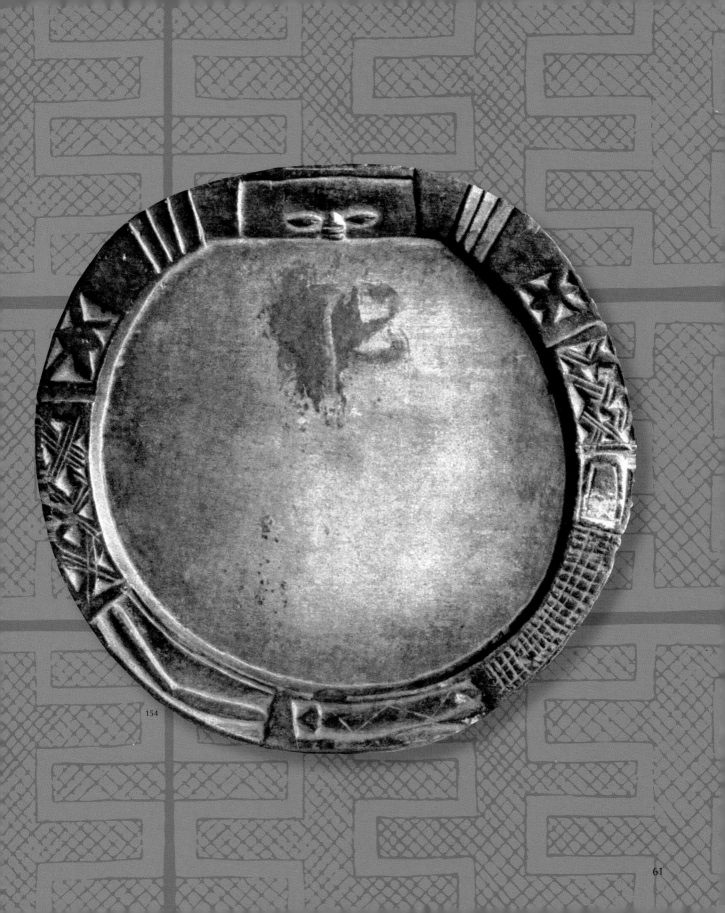

154

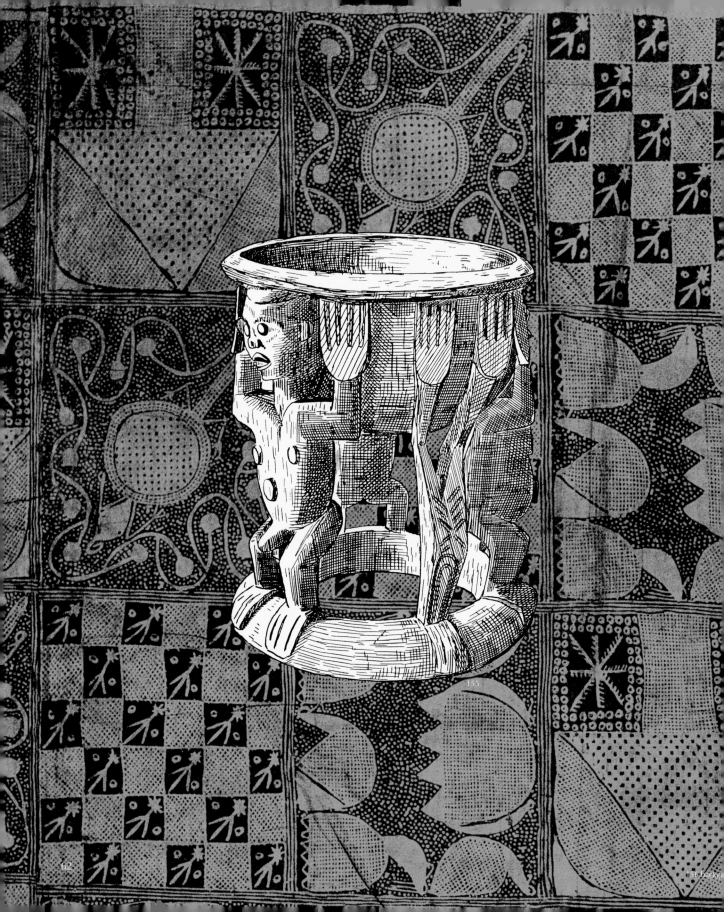

155

136 back

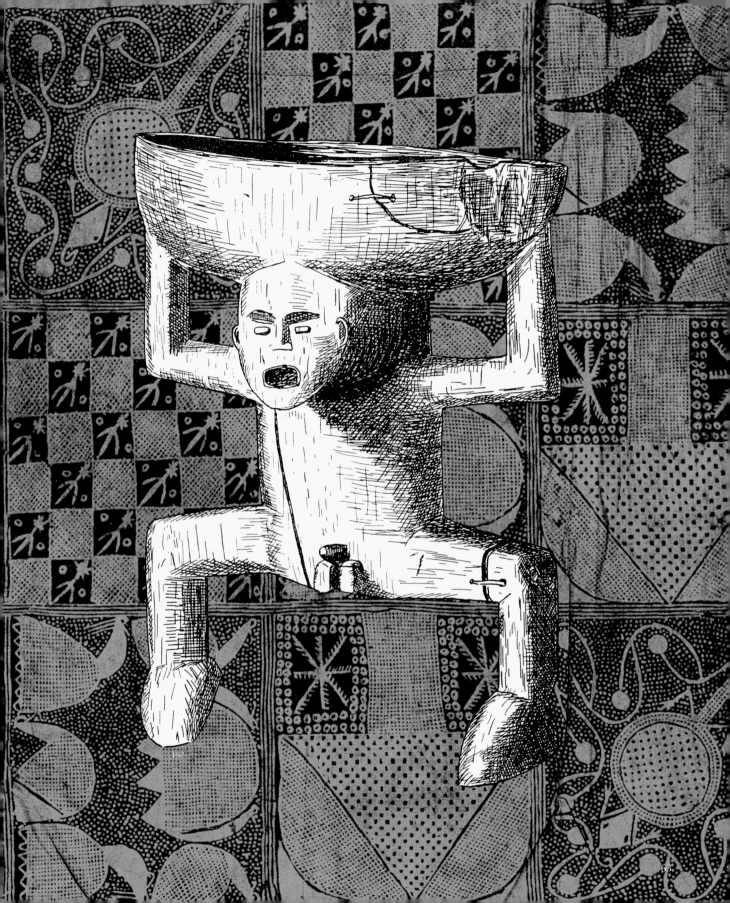

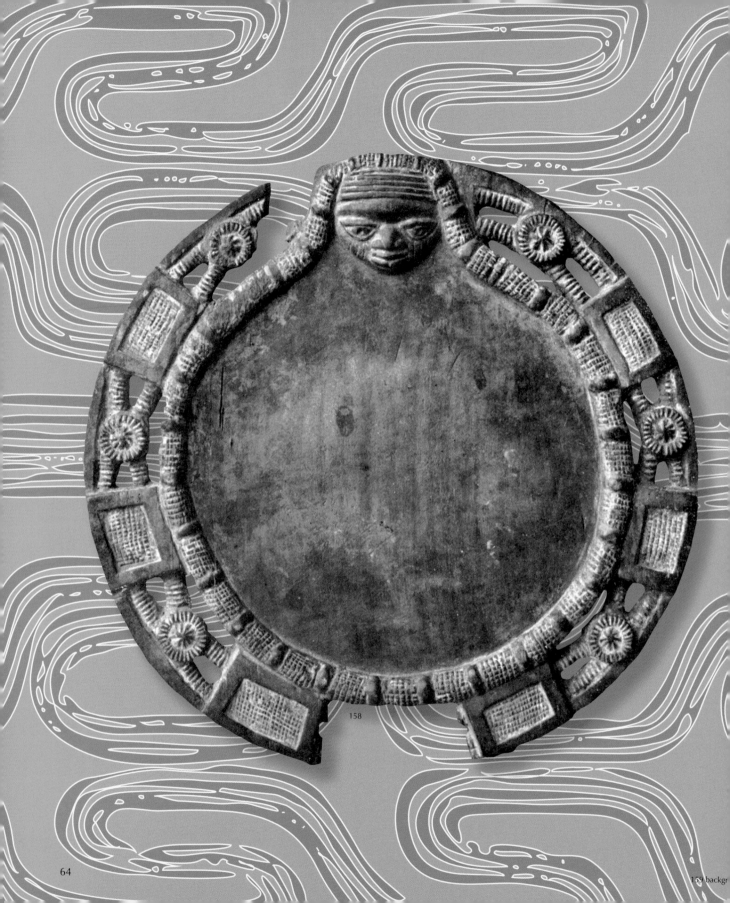

158

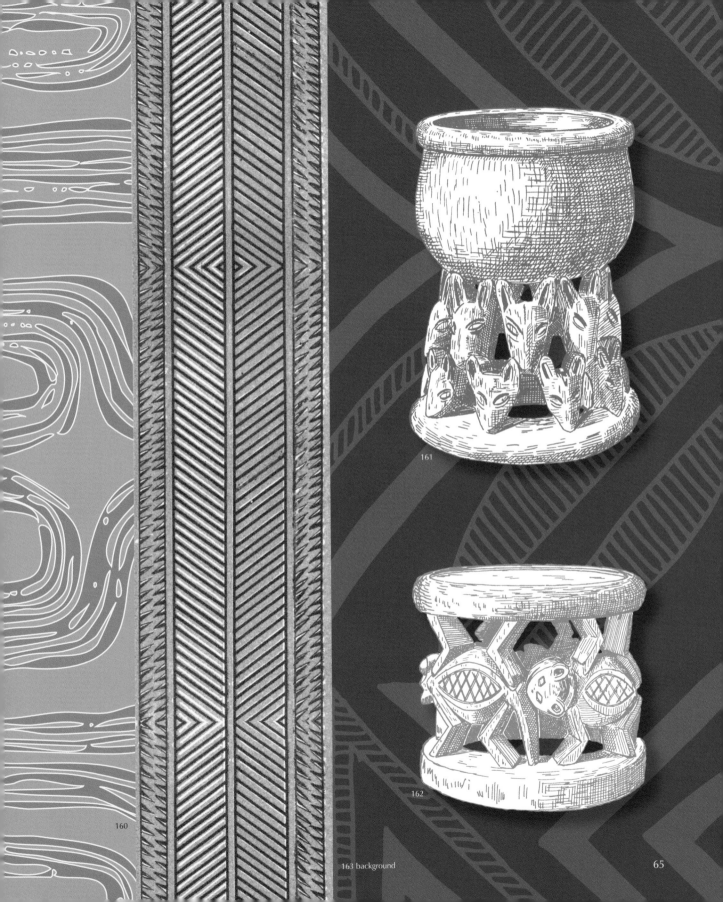

160

161

162

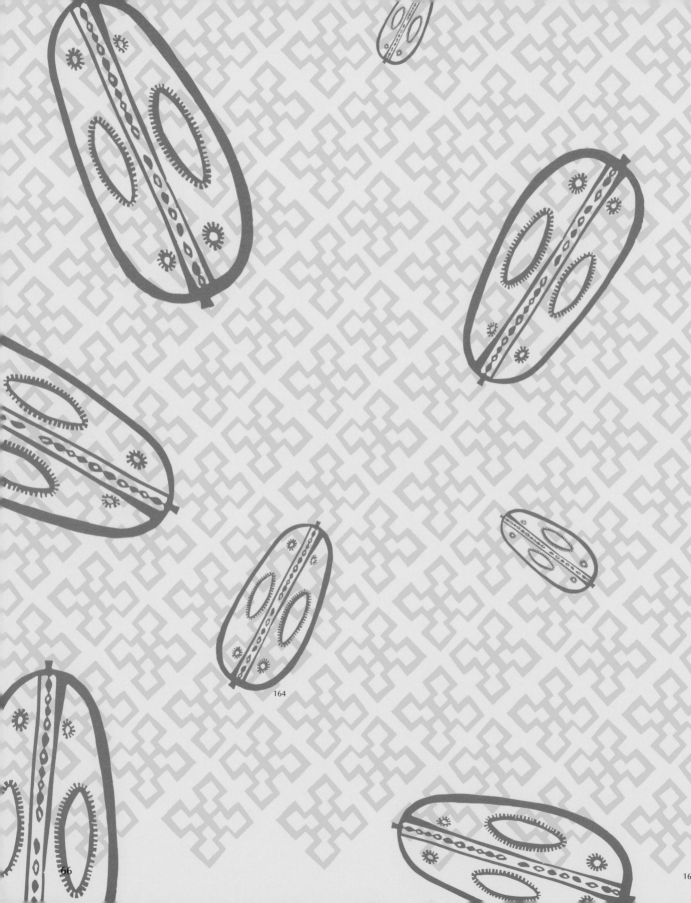

164

165 backgr

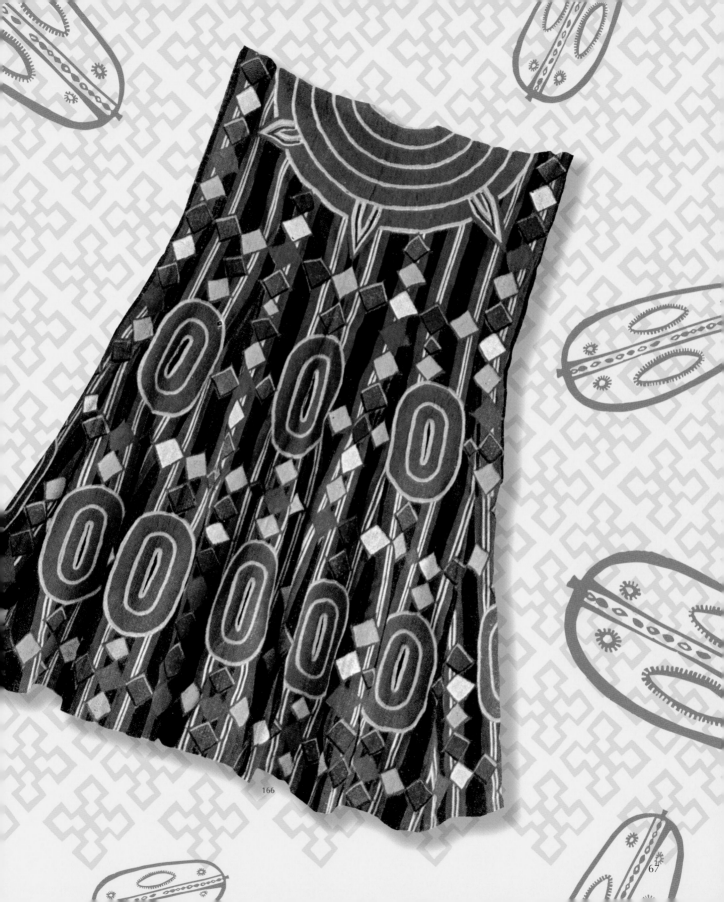

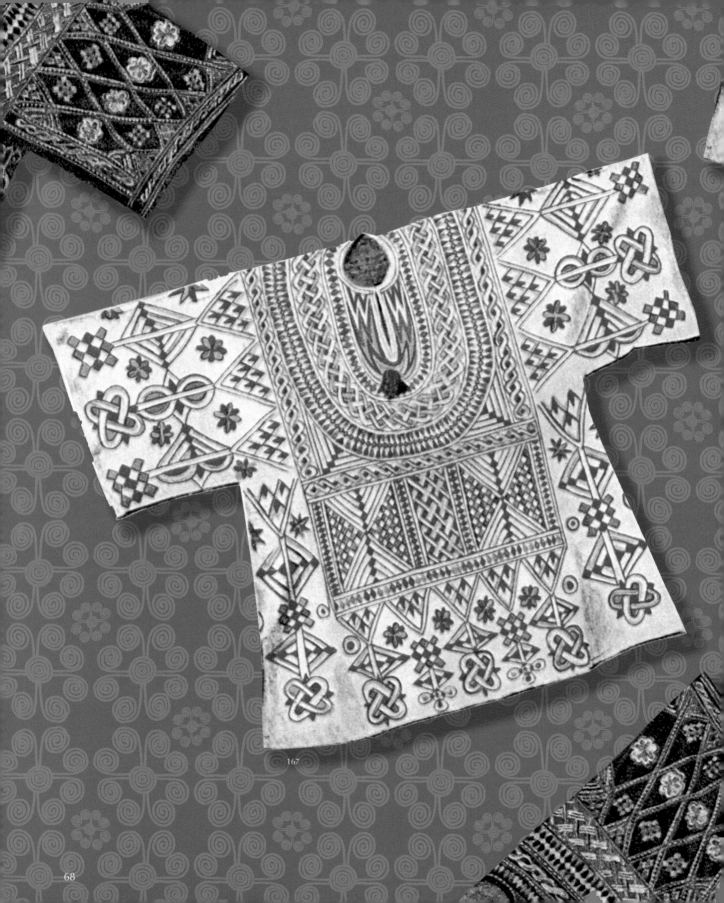

167

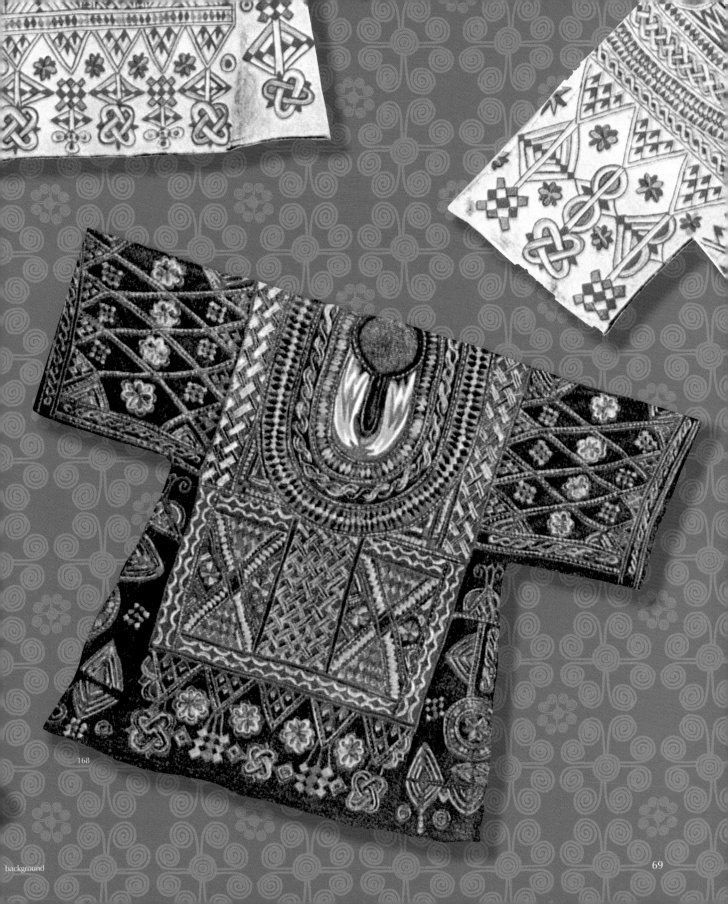

168

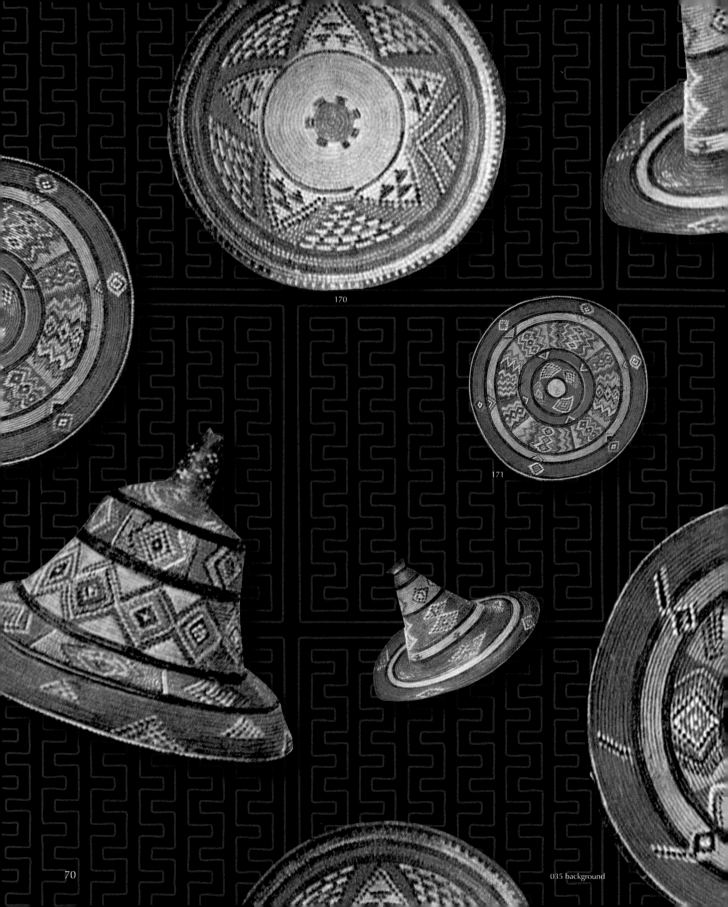

170

171

035 background

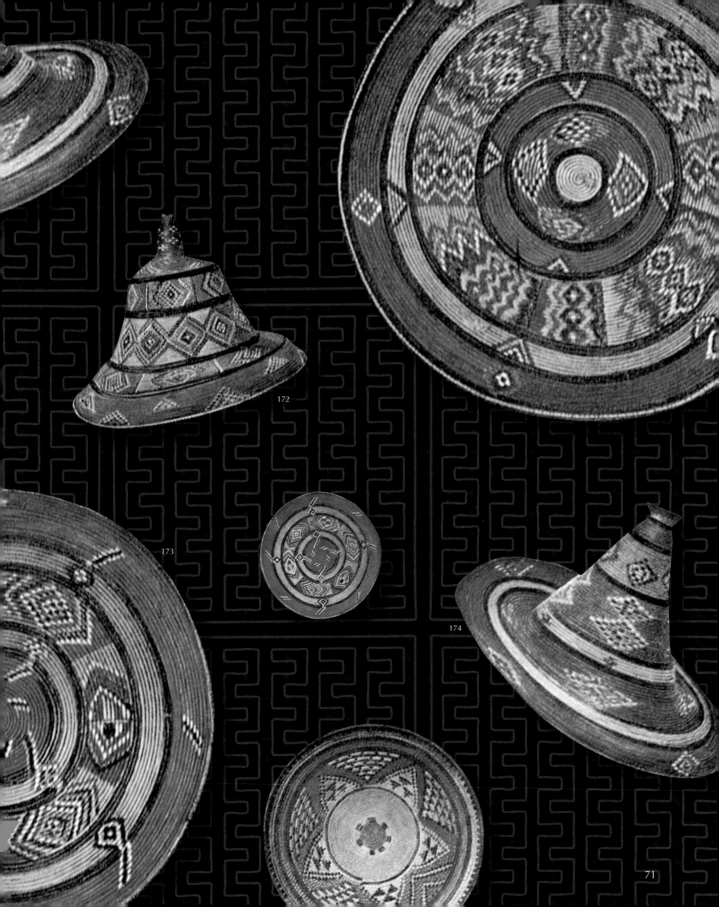

172

173

174

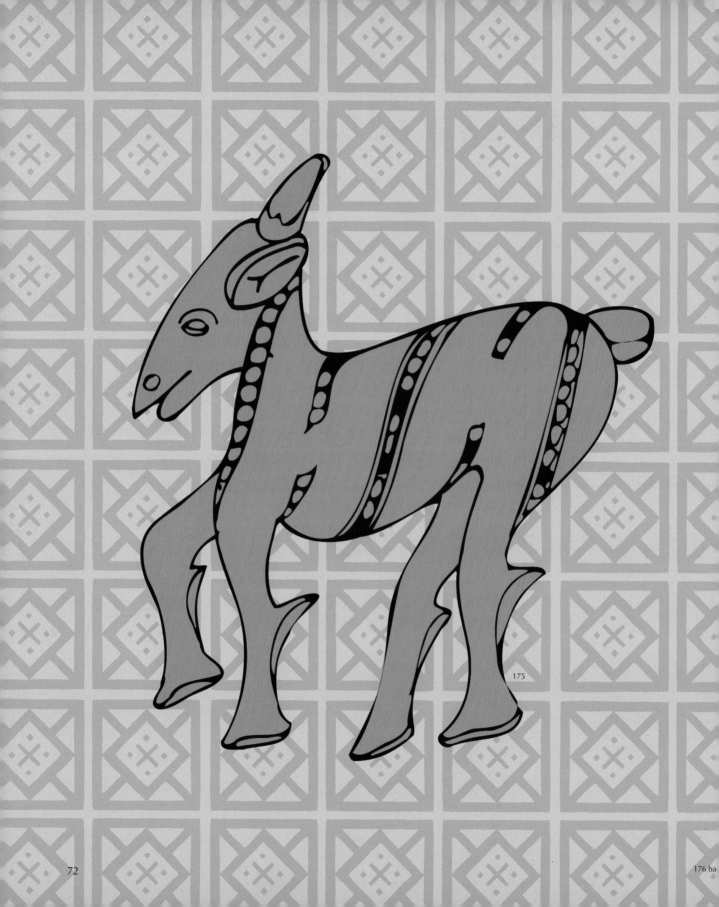

175

176 ba

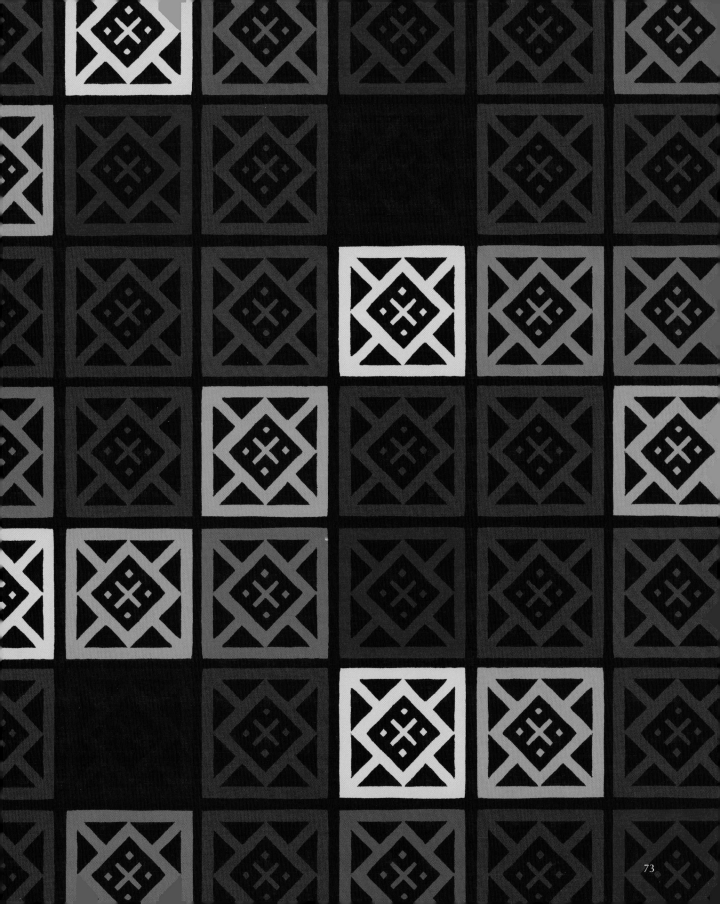

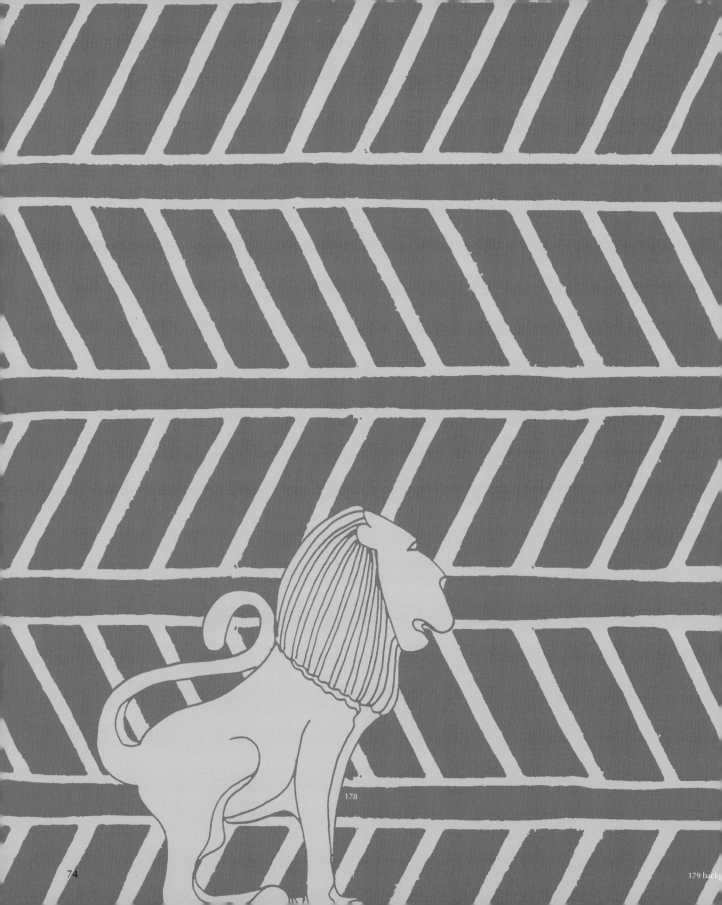

178

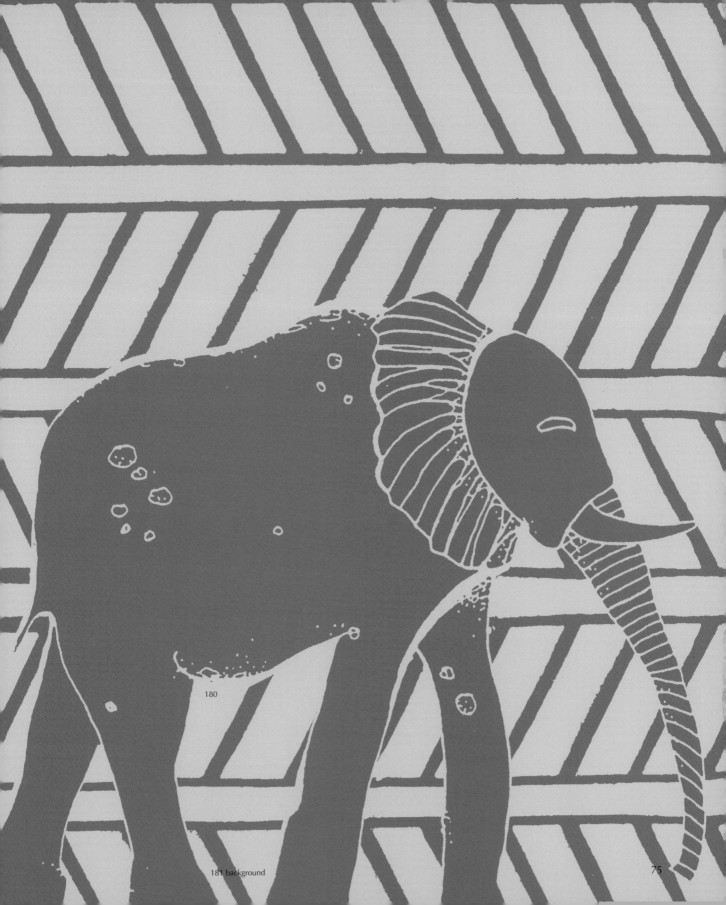

180

181 background

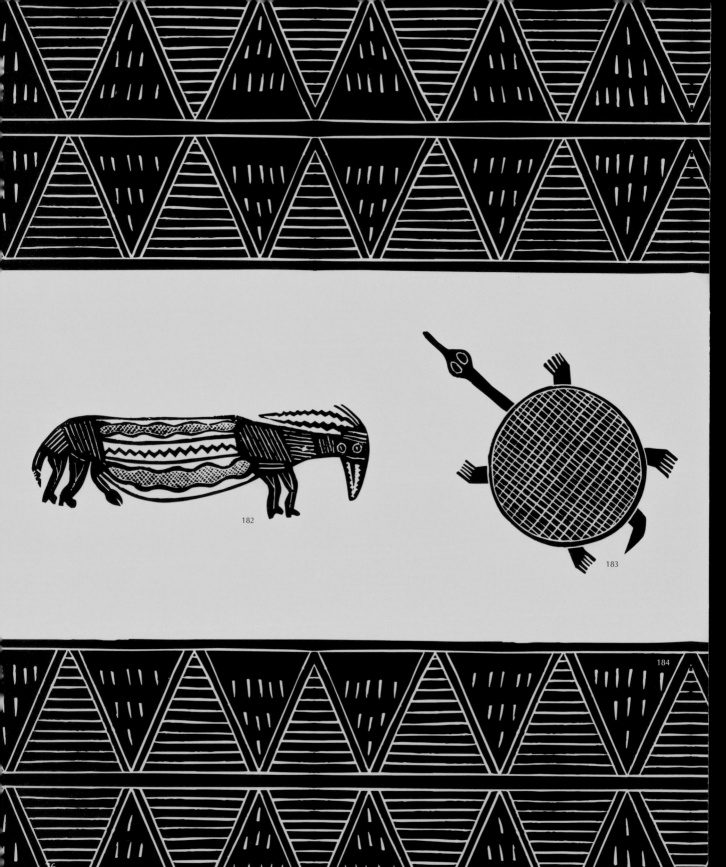

182

183

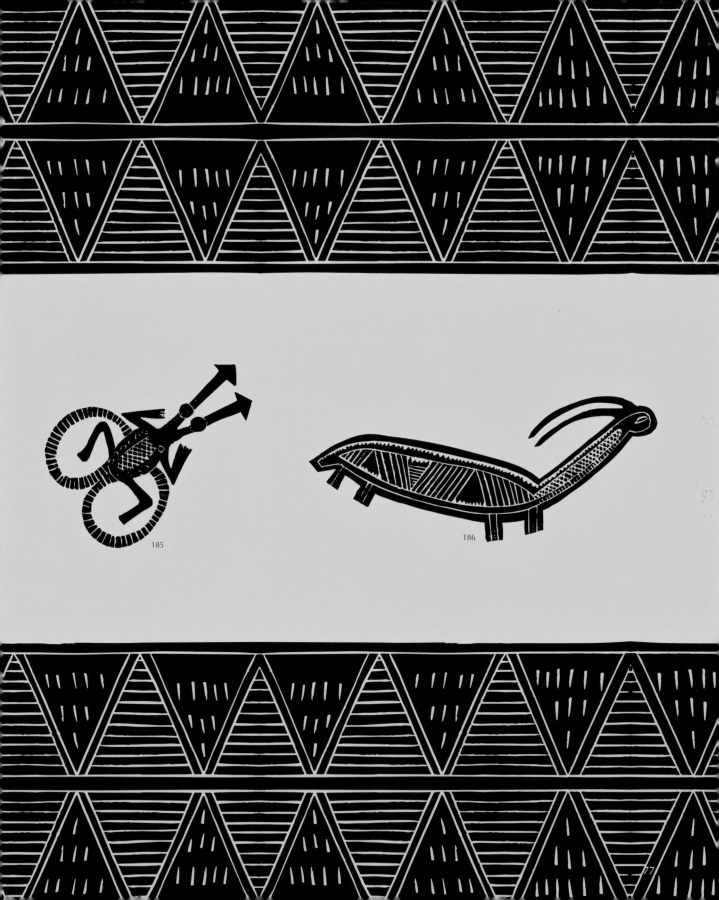

185

186

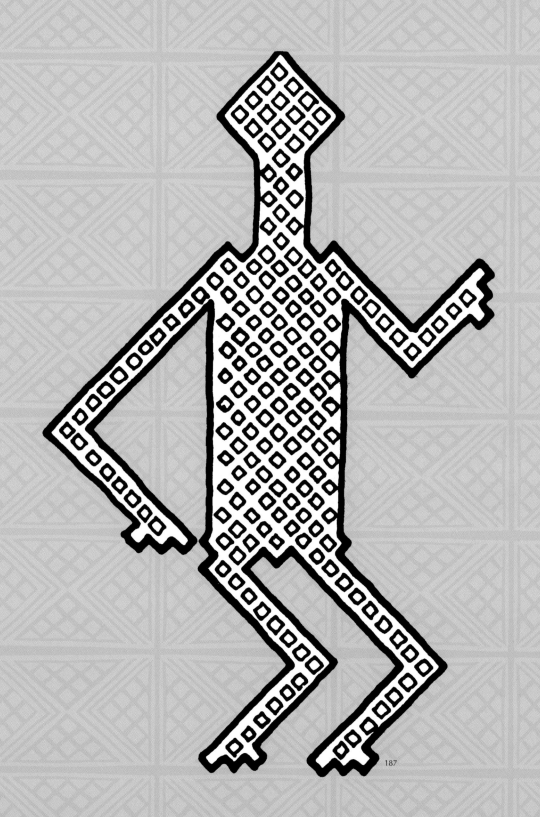

187

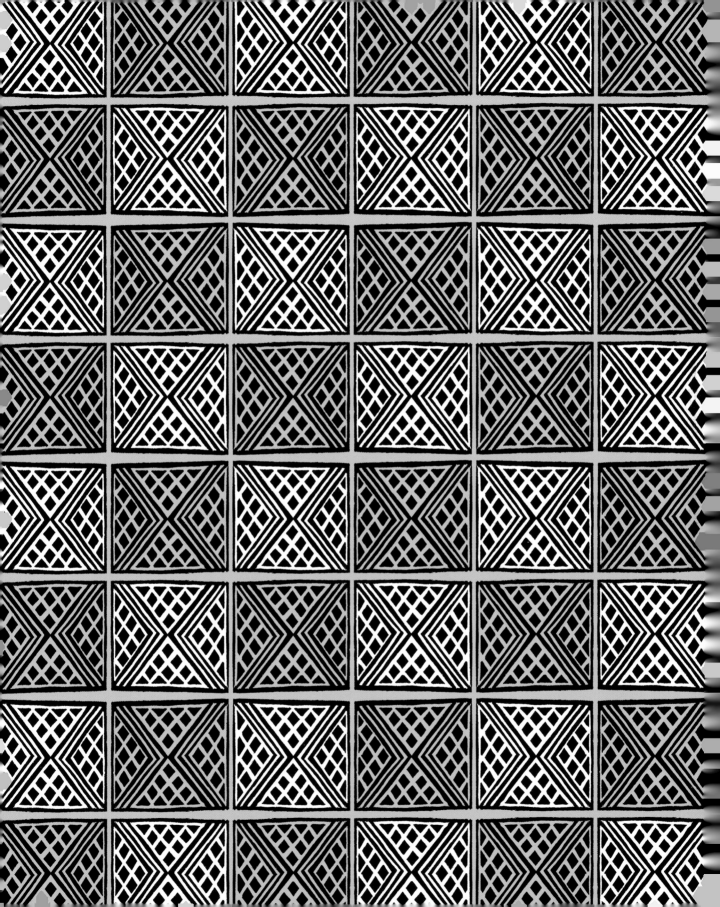

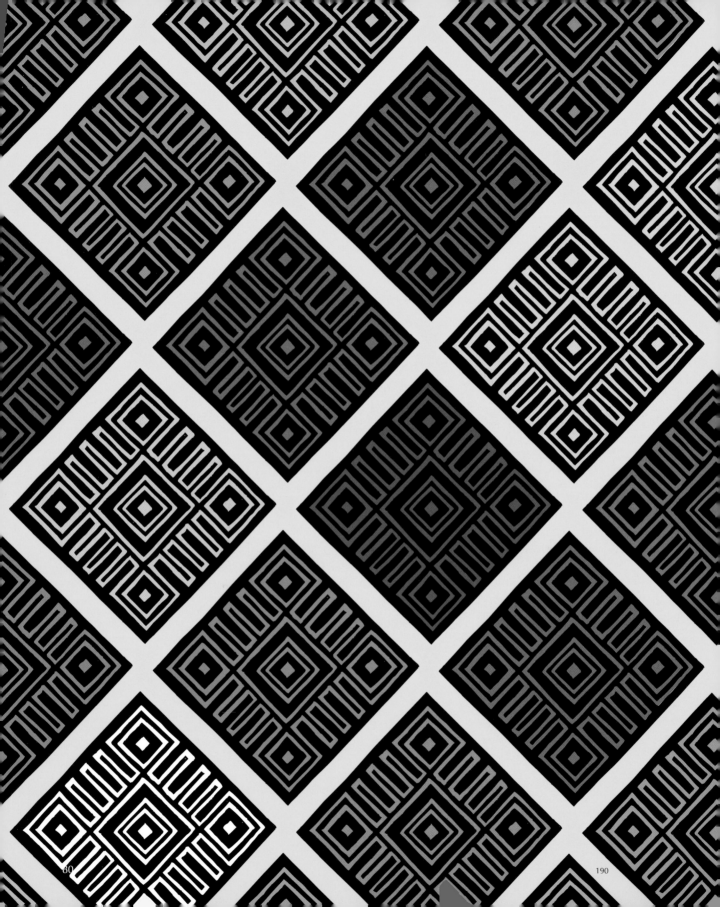

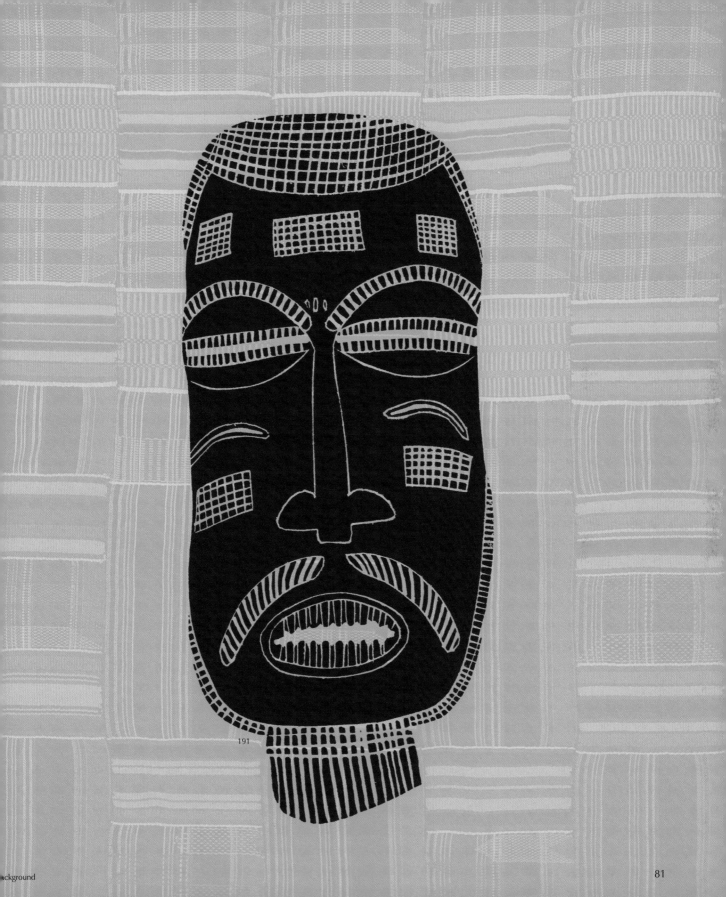

191

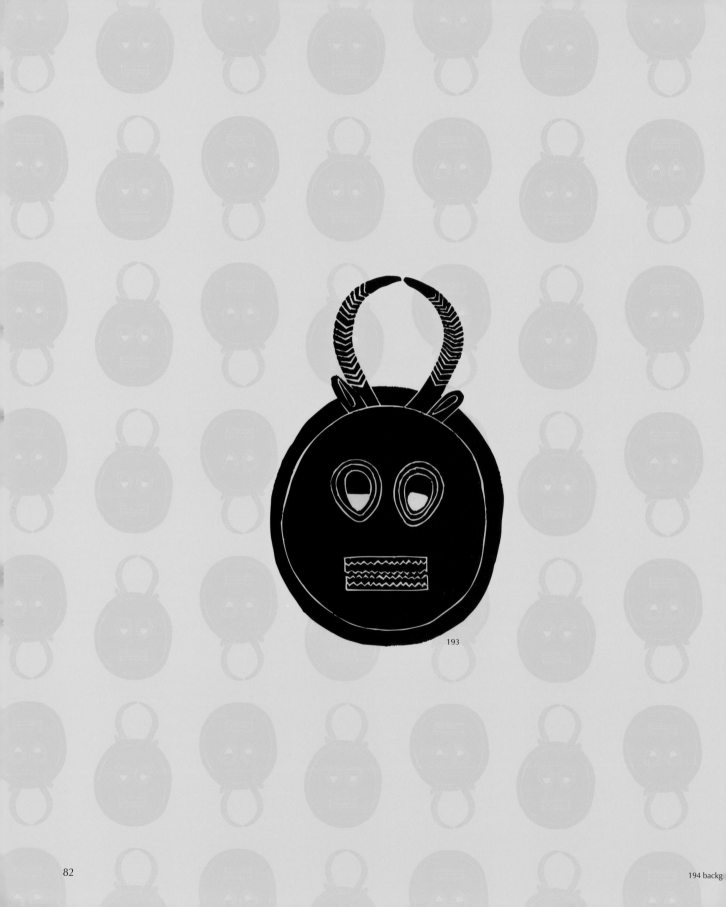

193

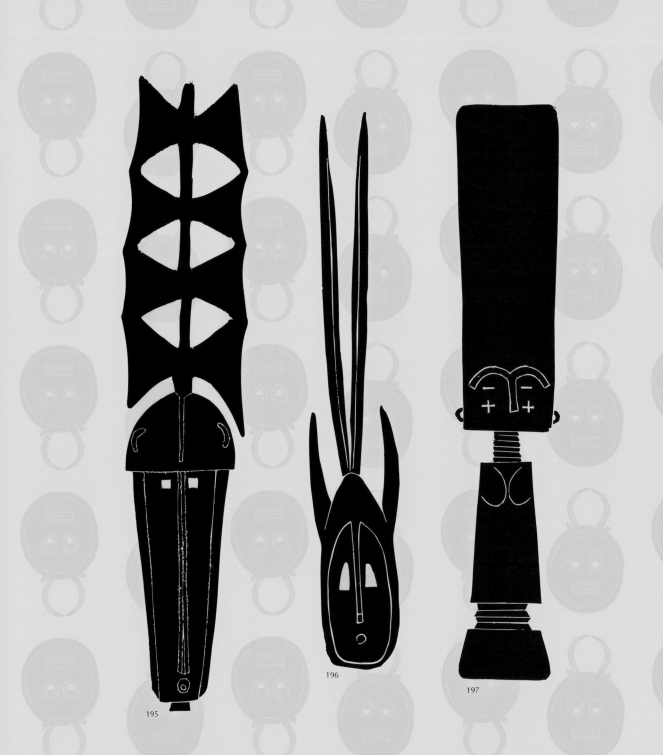

195

196

197

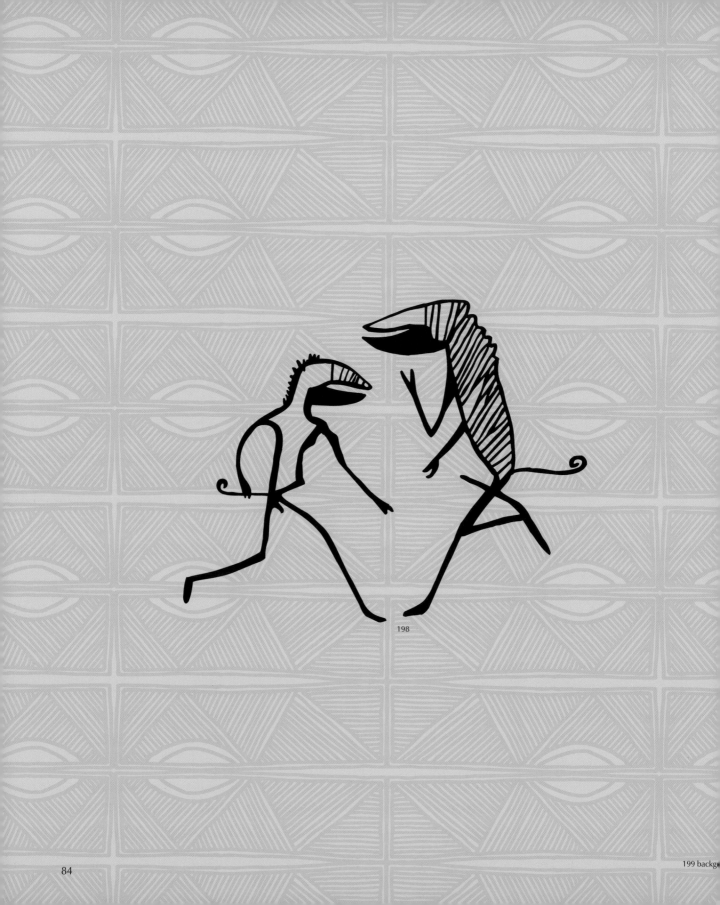

198

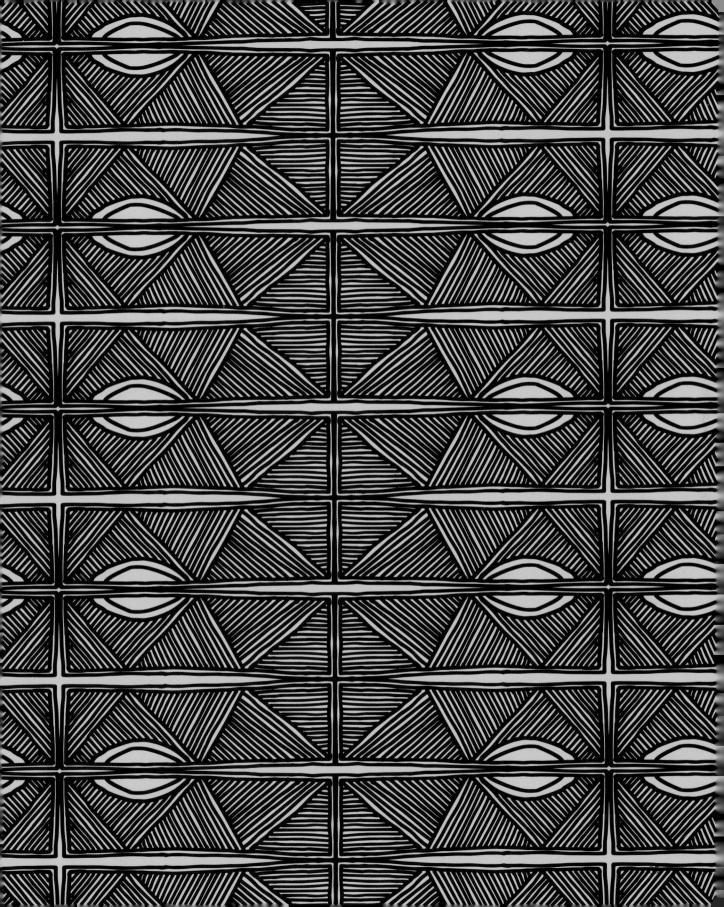

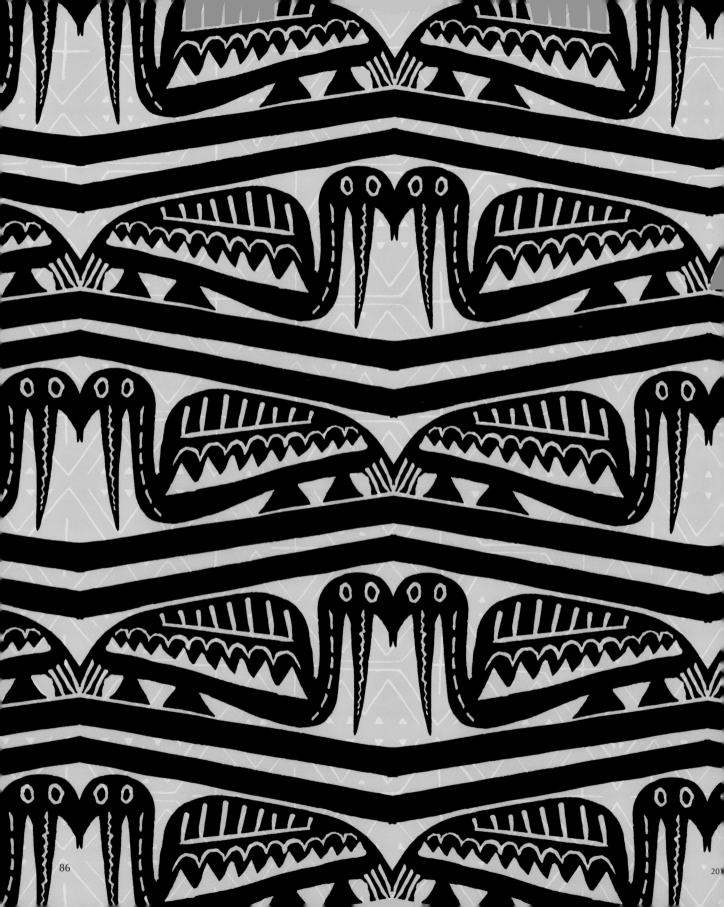

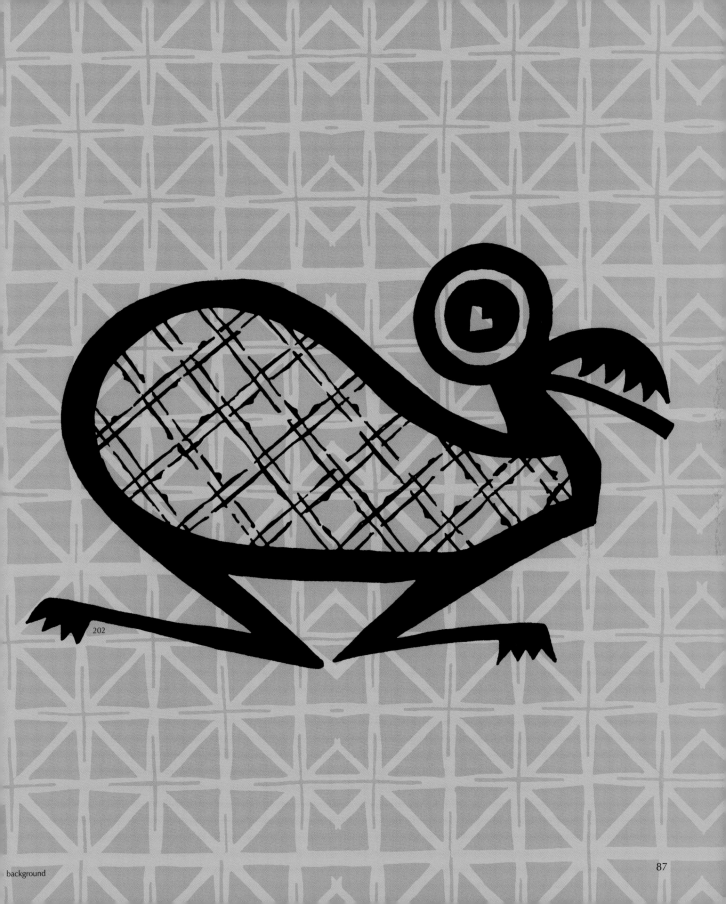

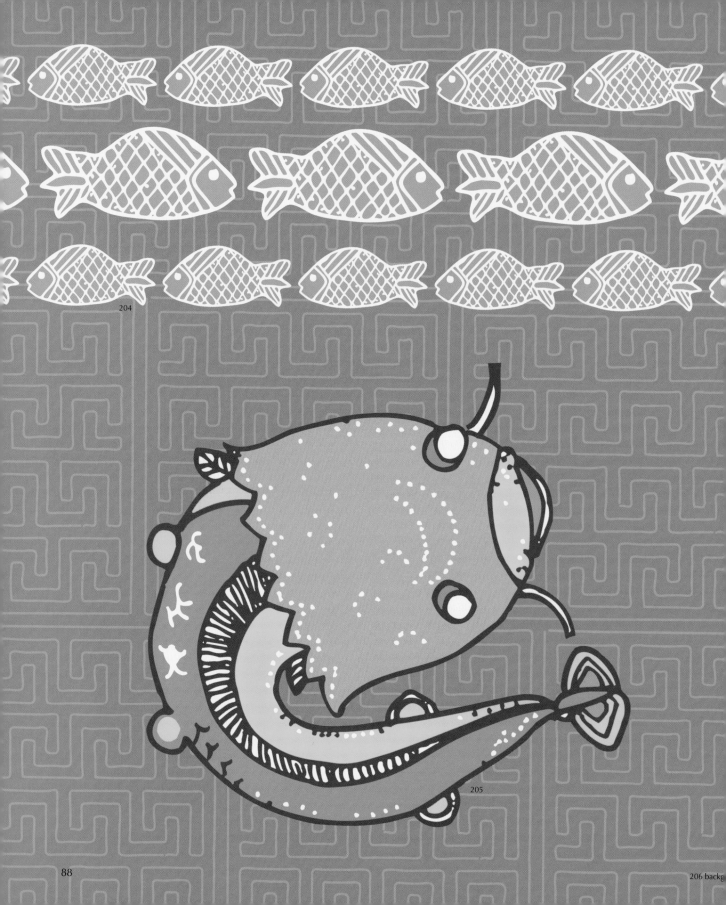

204

205

206 backg

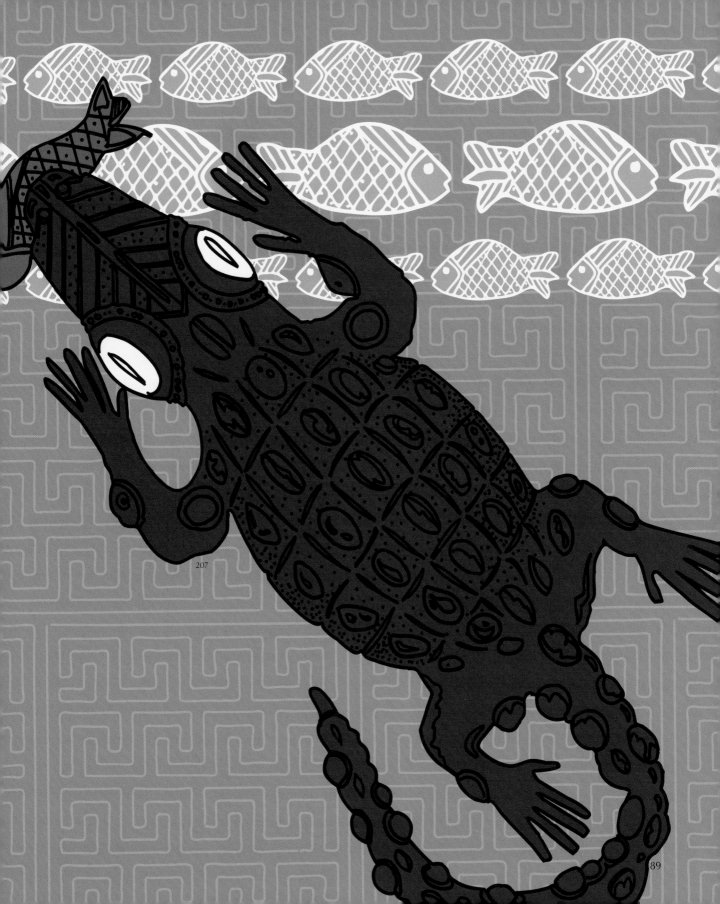

207

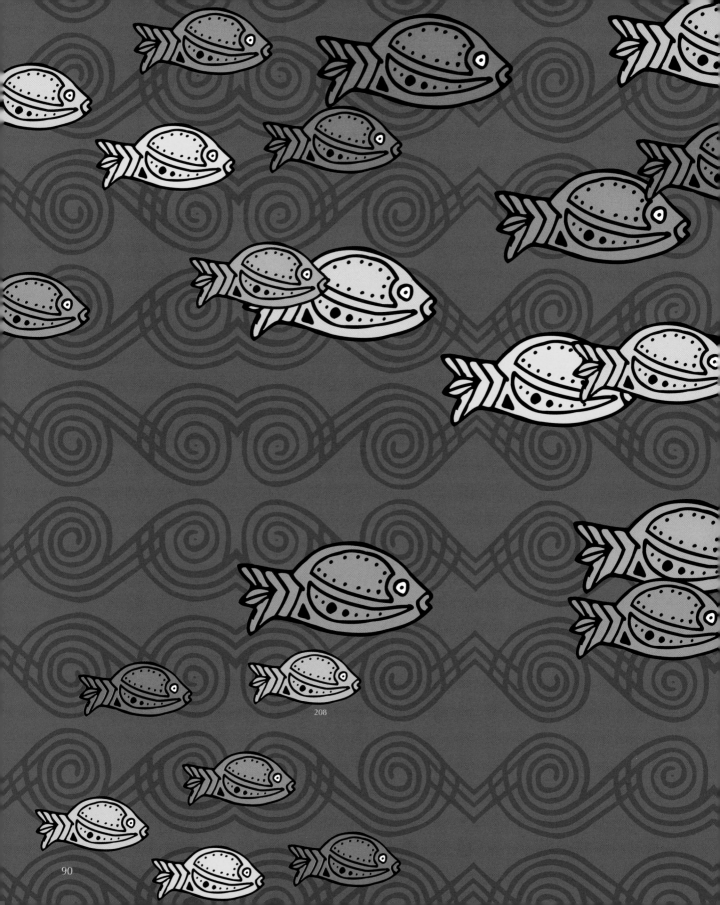

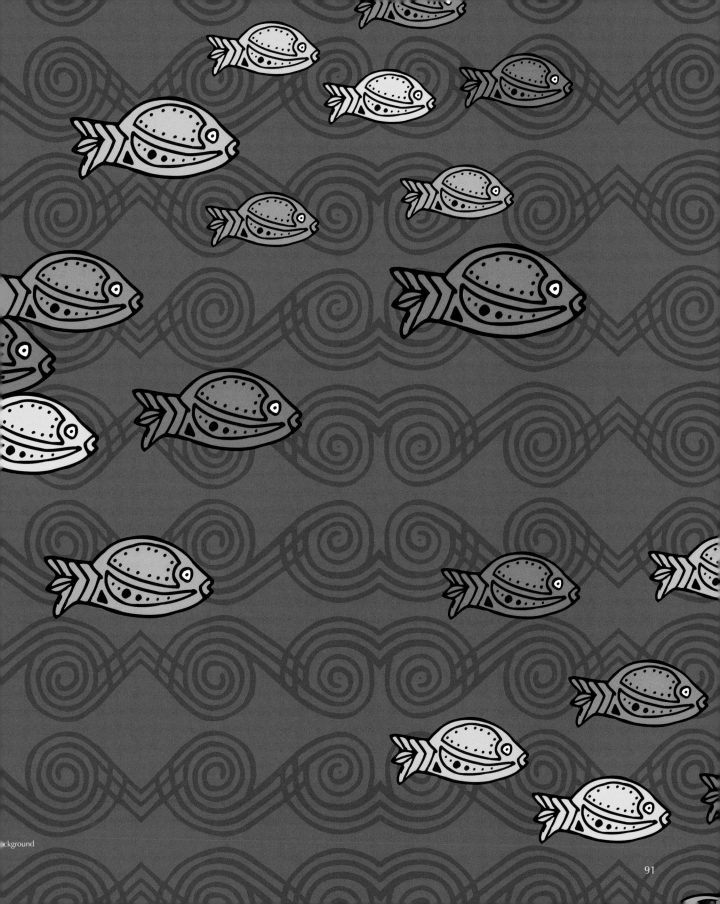

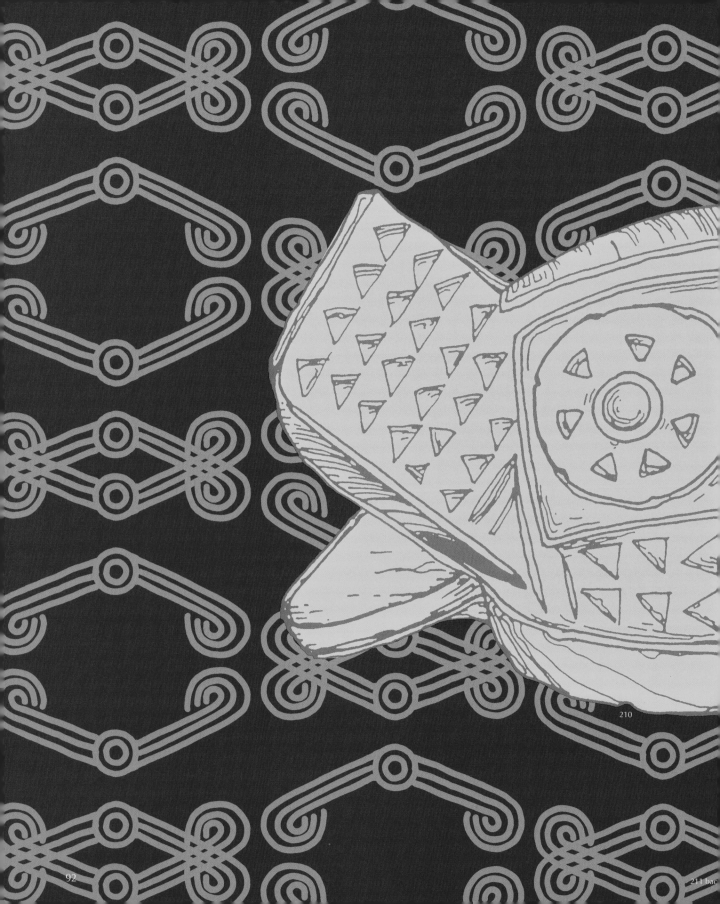

210

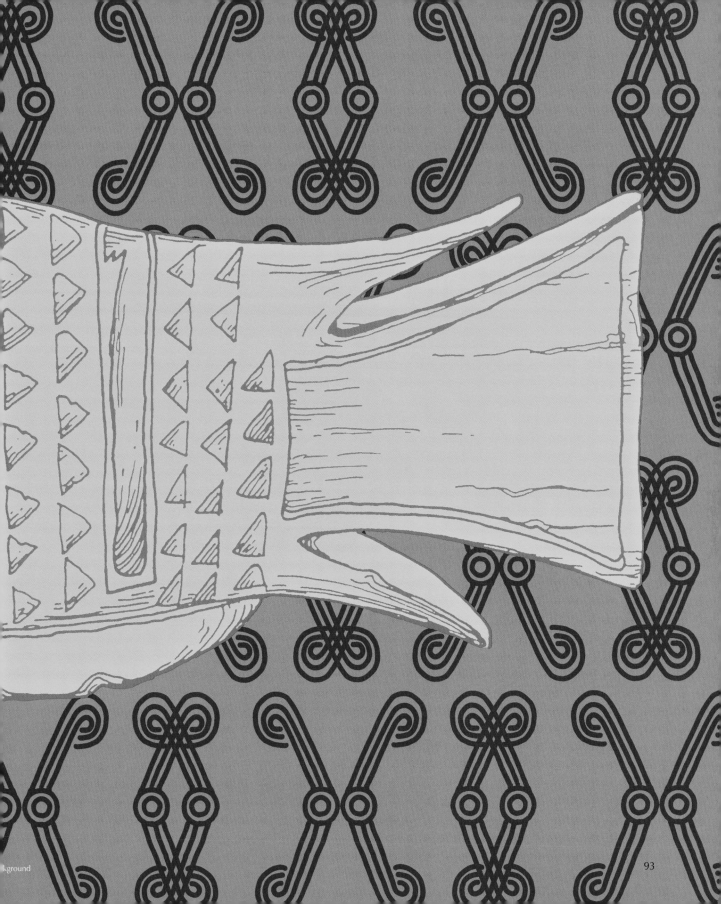

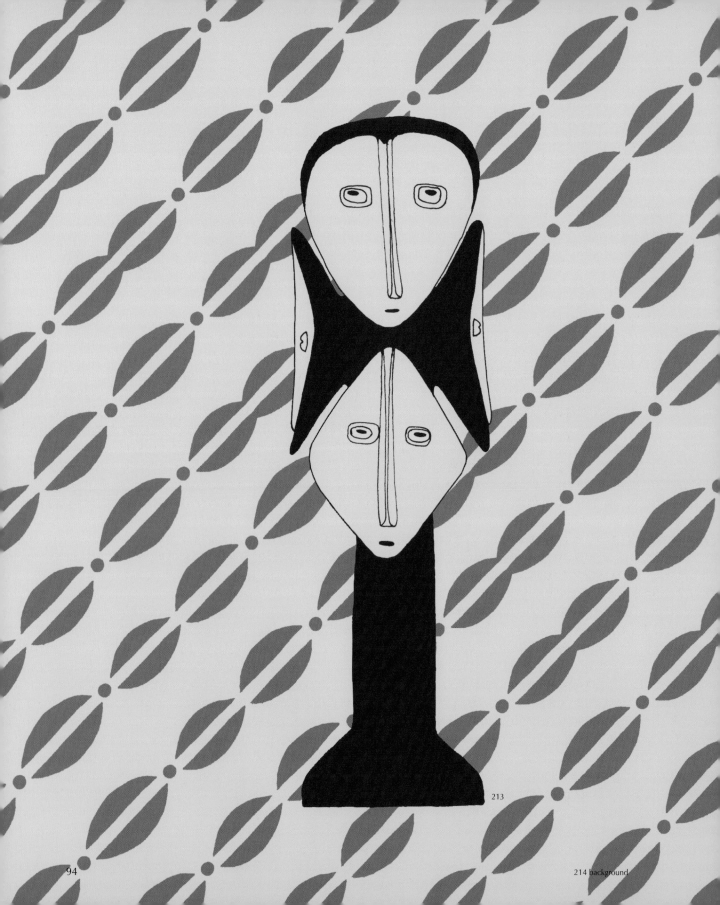

213

214 background

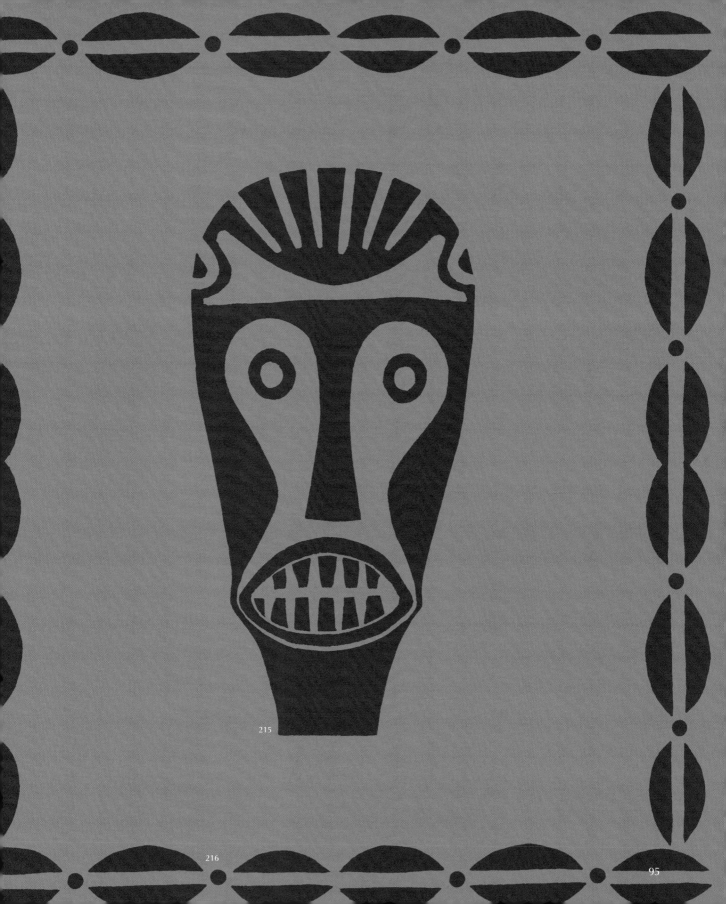

215

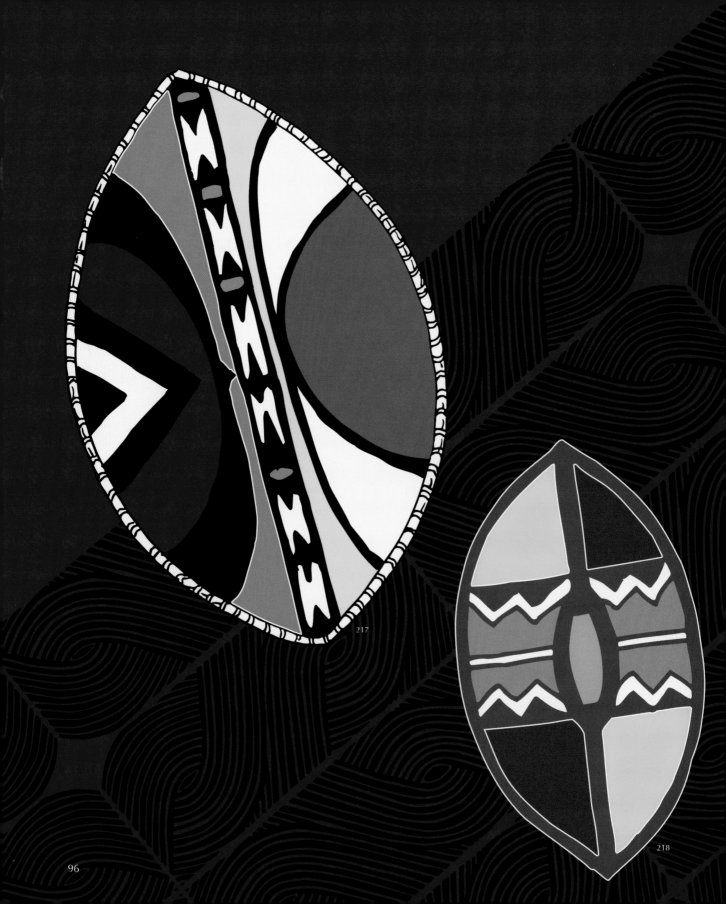

217

218

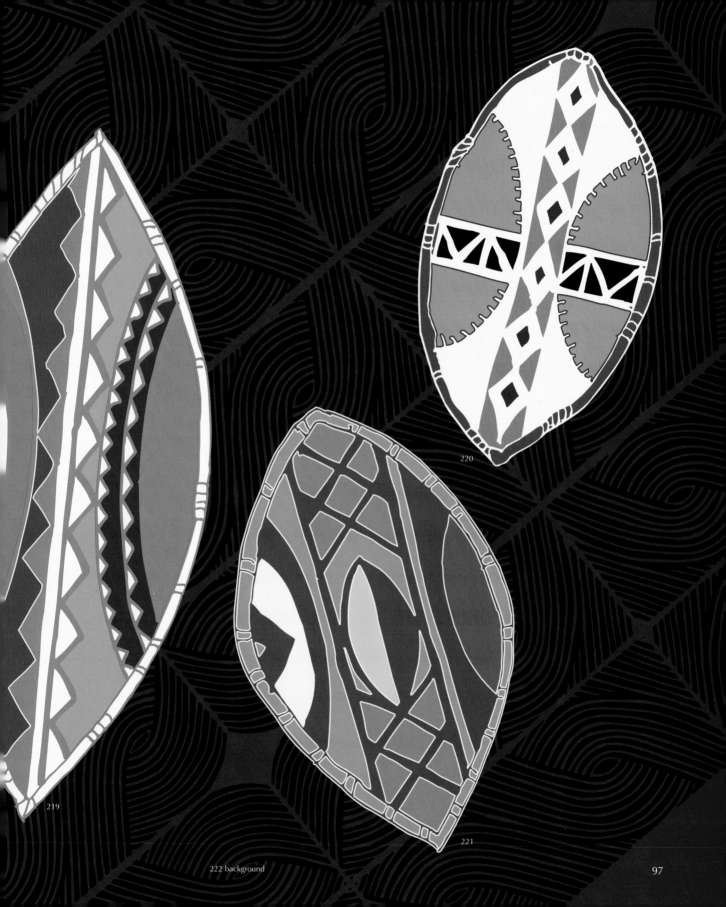

219

220

221

223

224

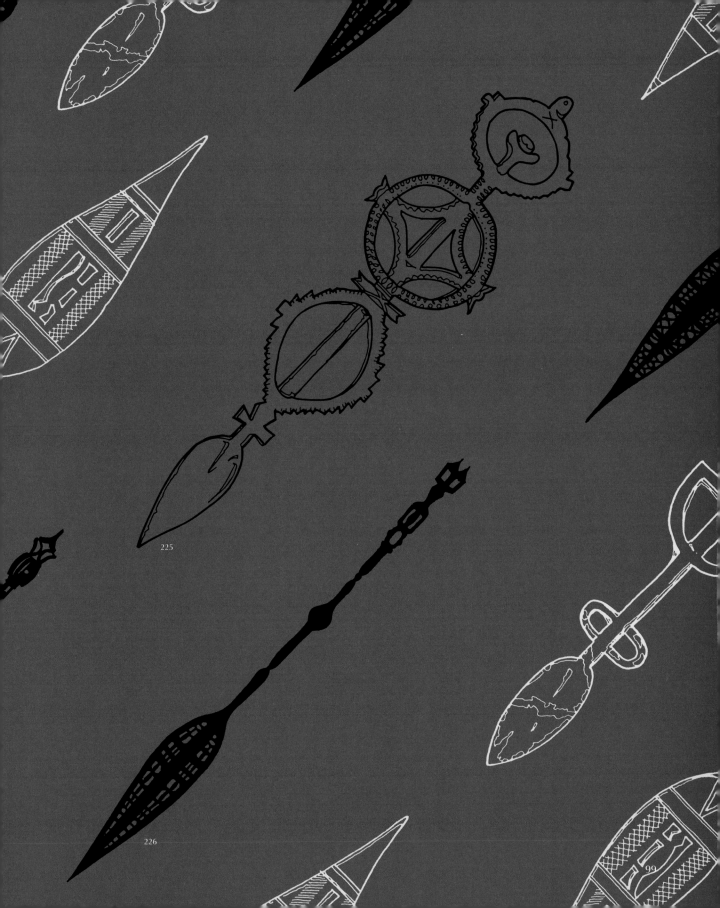

225

226

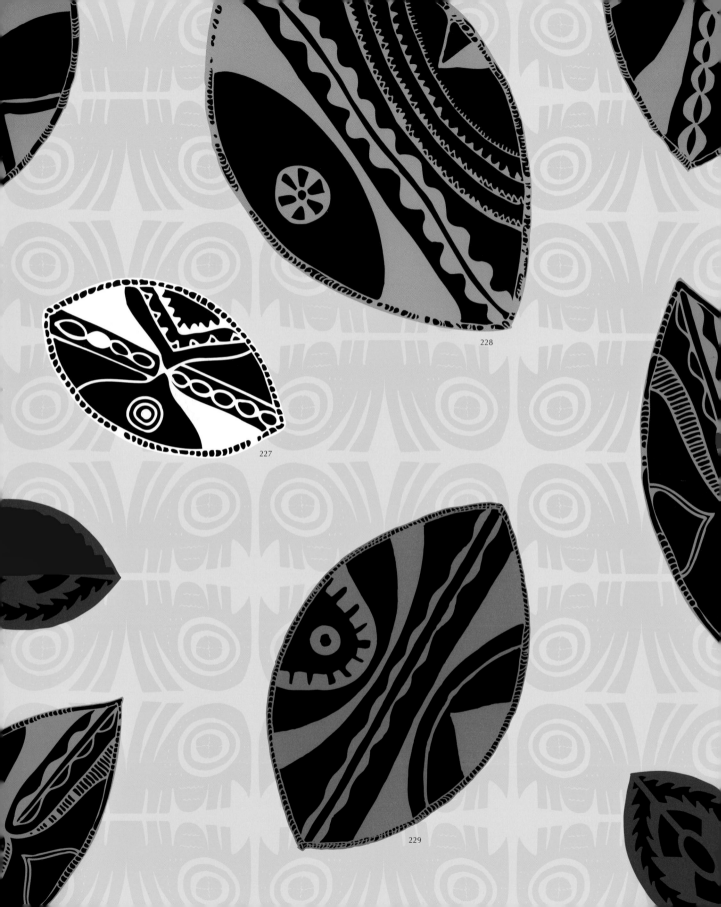

227

228

229

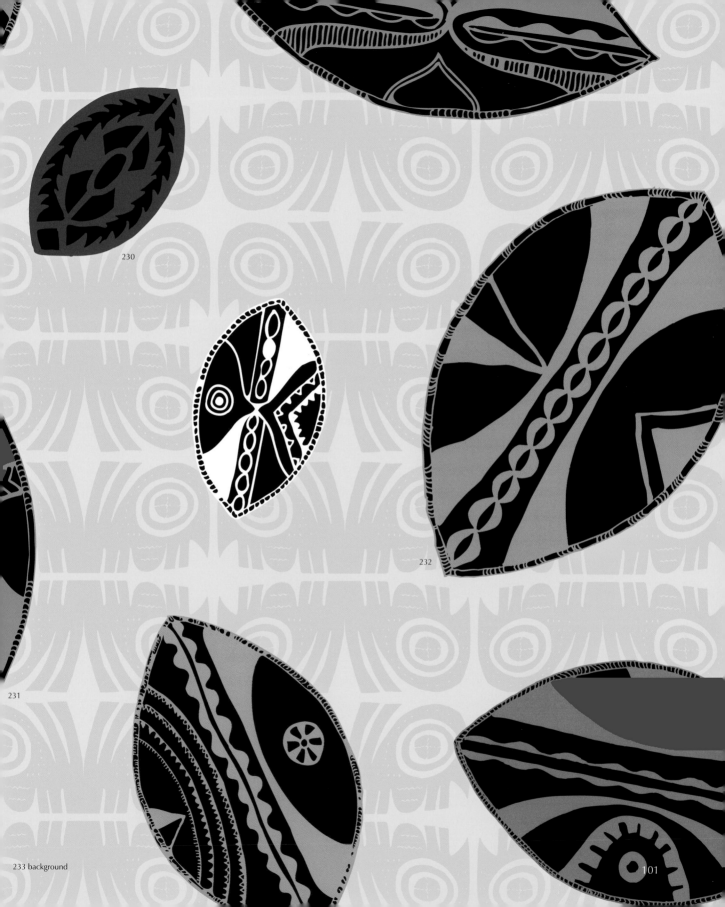

230

232

231

233 background

101

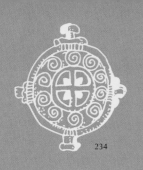

234

236

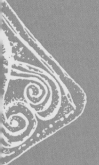

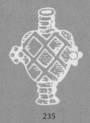

235

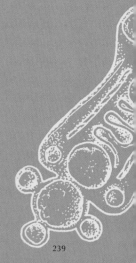

239

237

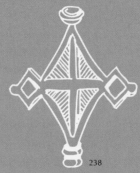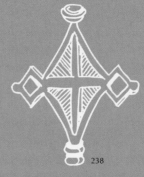

238

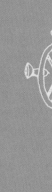

241

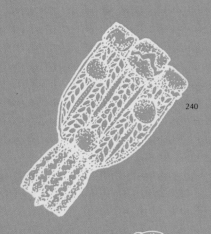

240

242

243

244

245

246

247

248

249

250

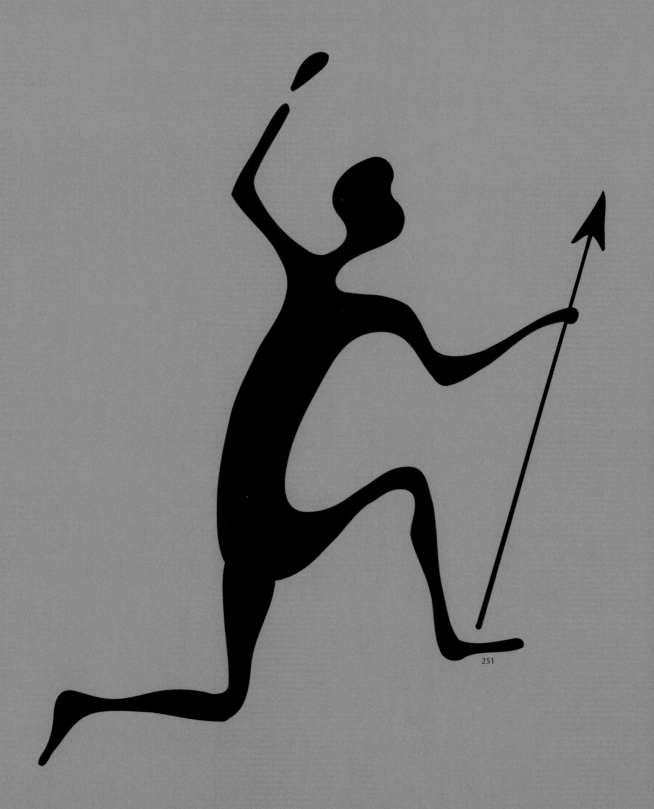

251

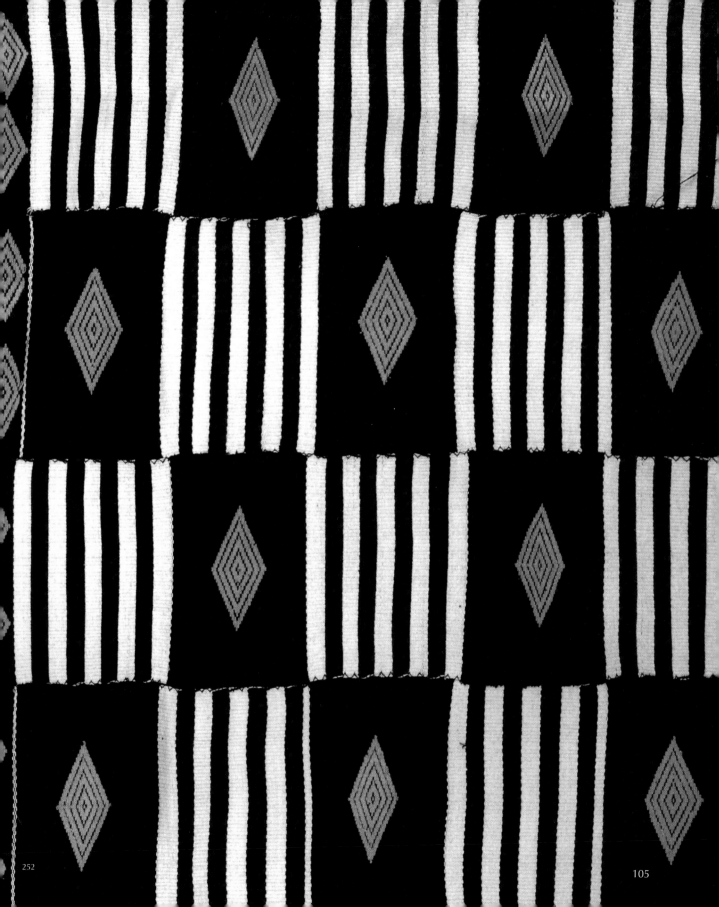

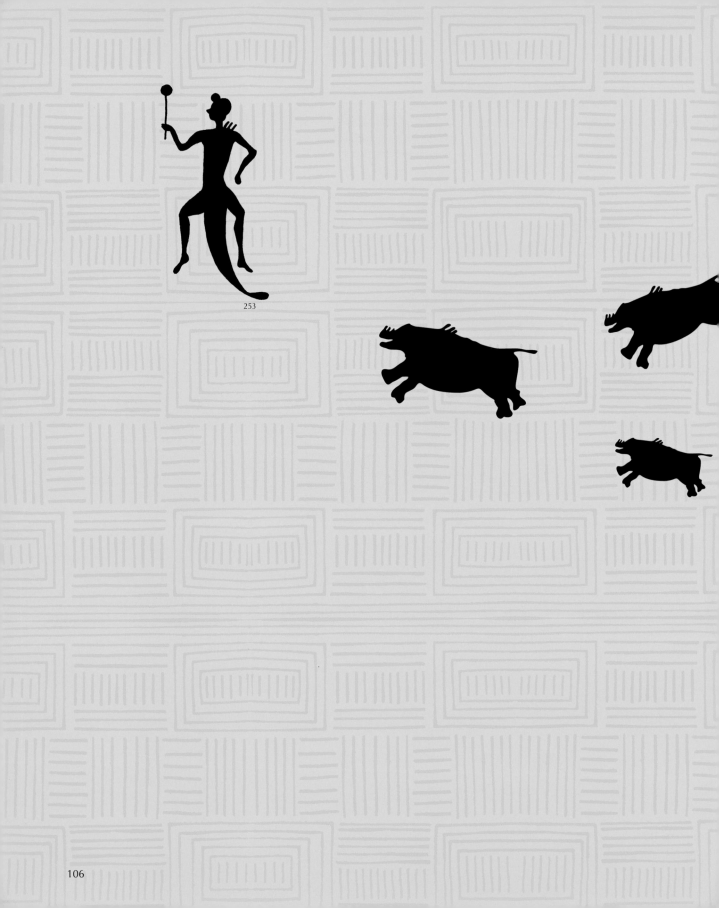

253

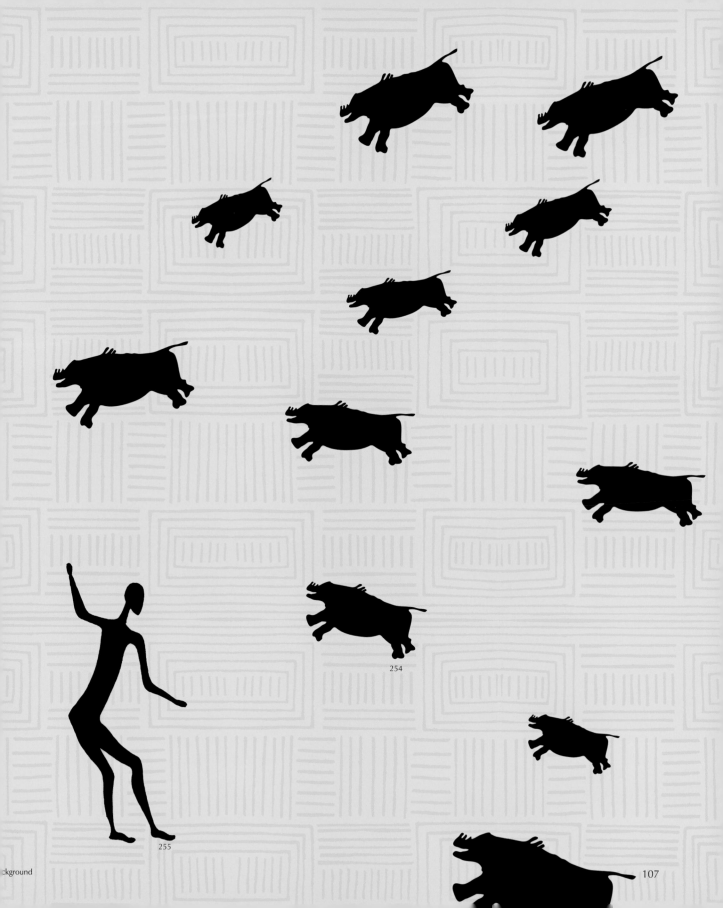

254

255

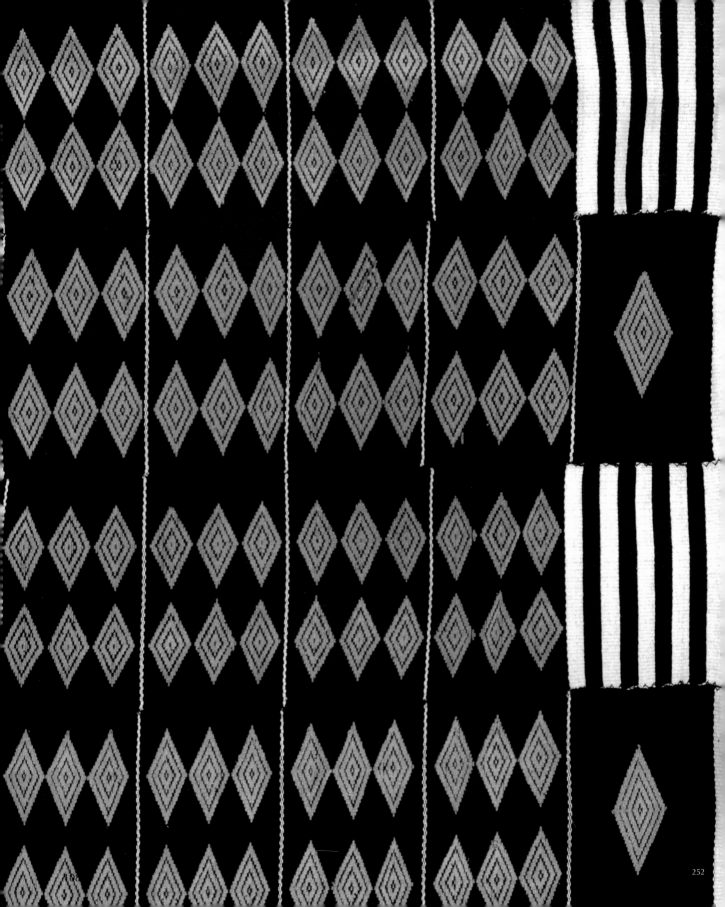

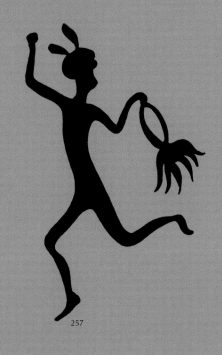

257

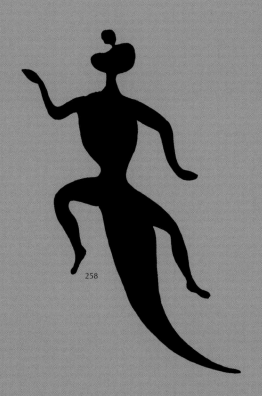

258

109

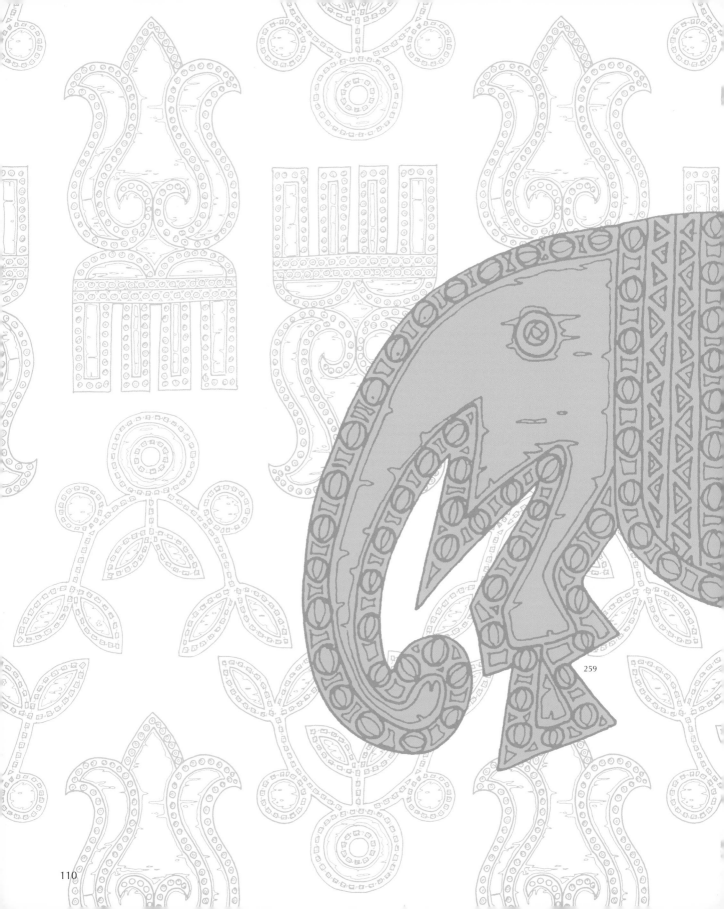

259

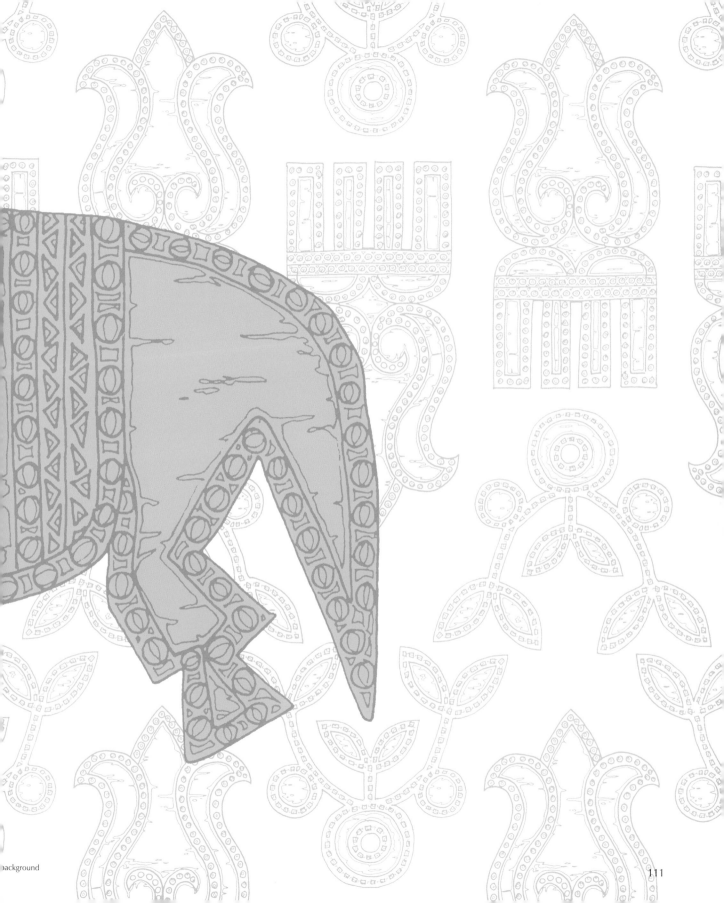

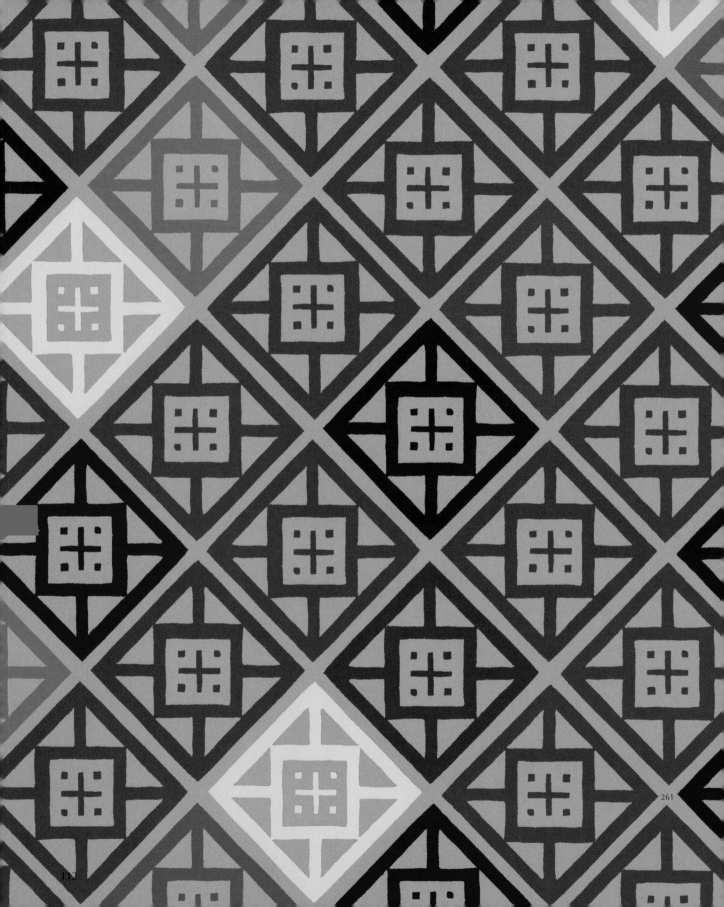

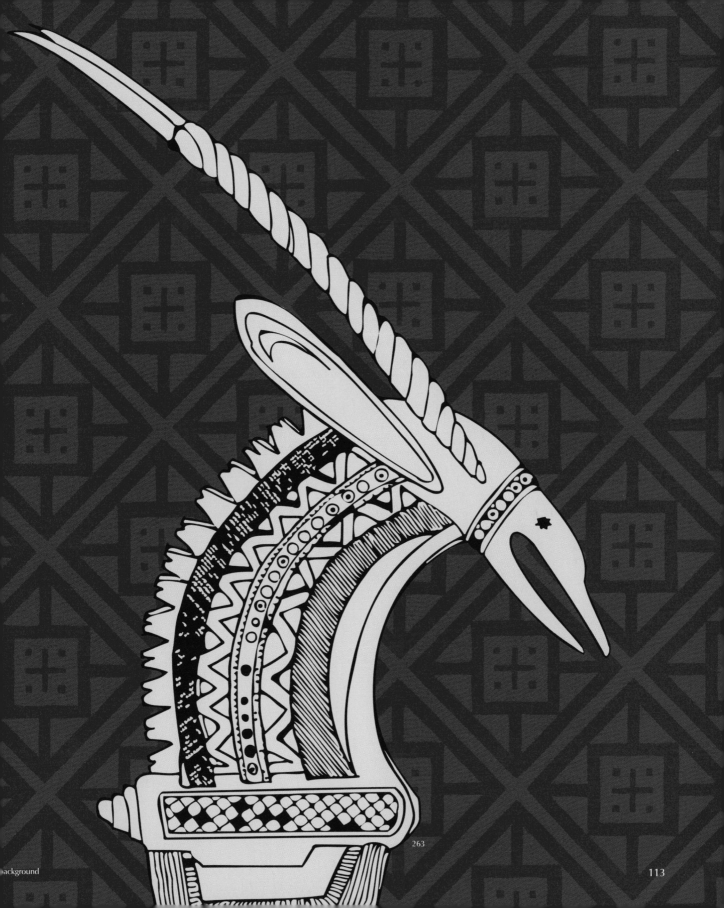

263

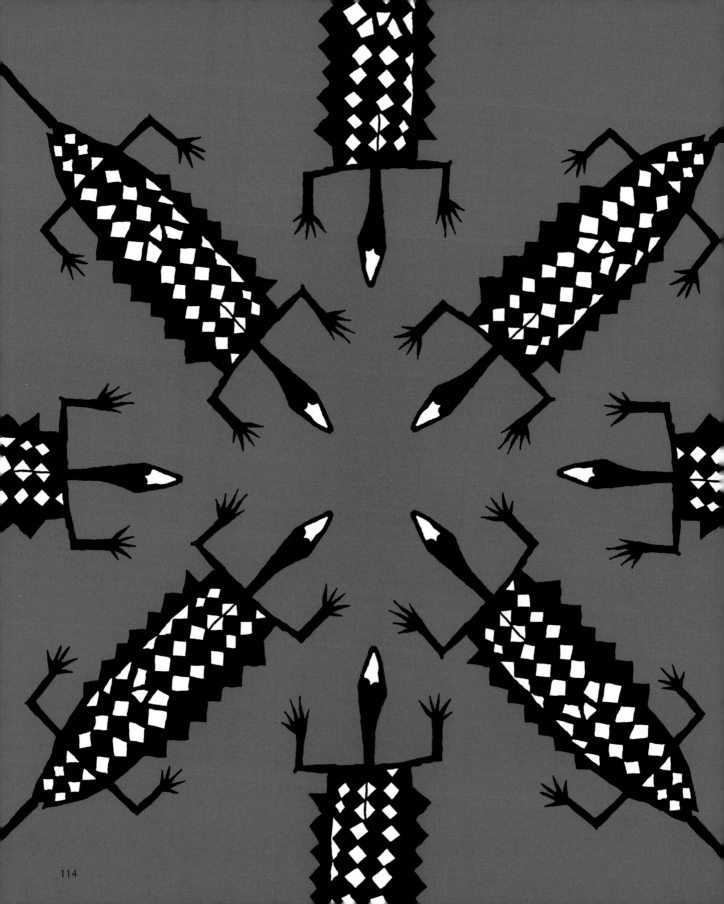

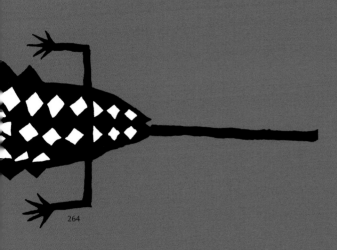

264

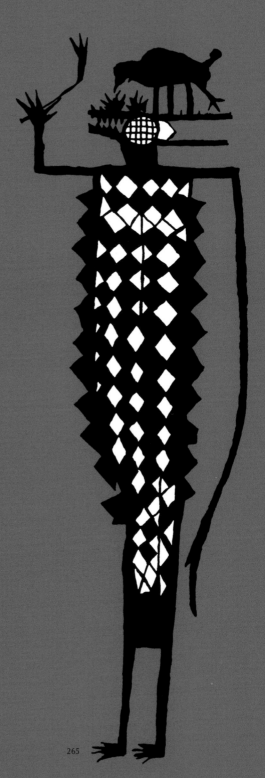

265

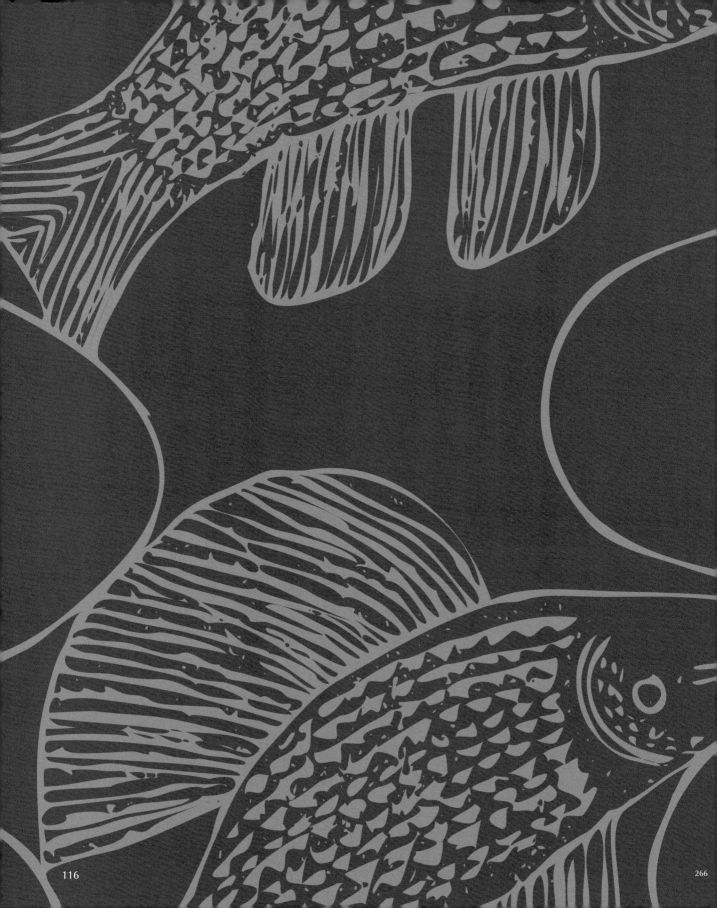

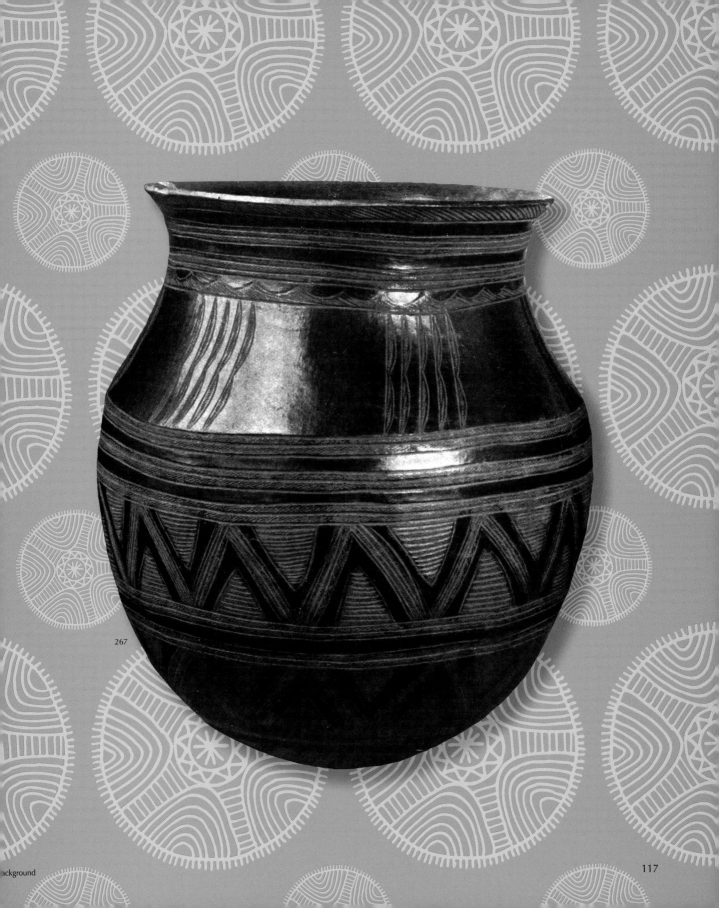

267

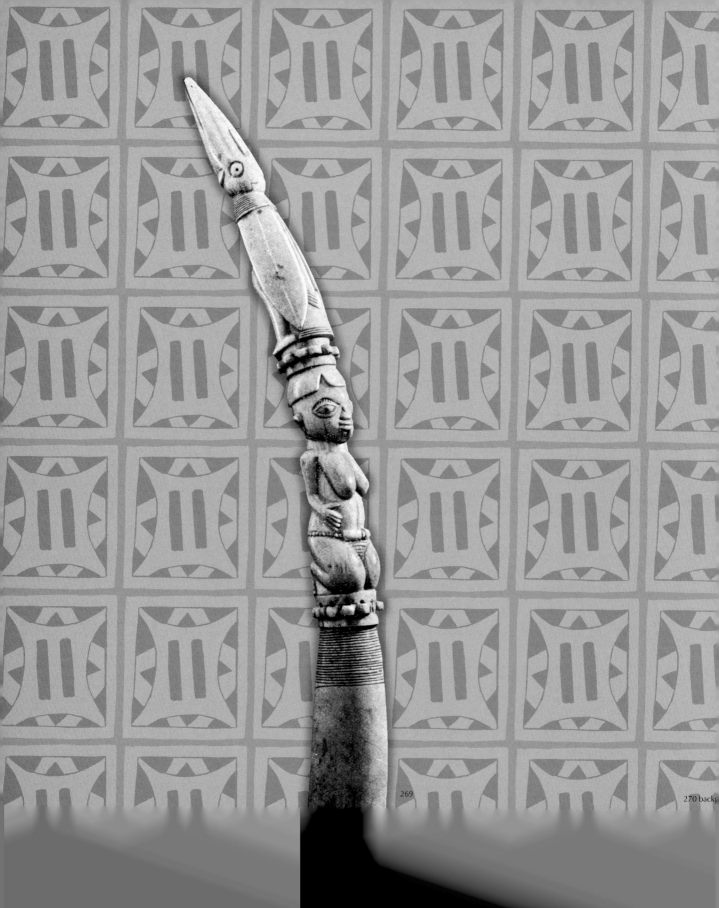

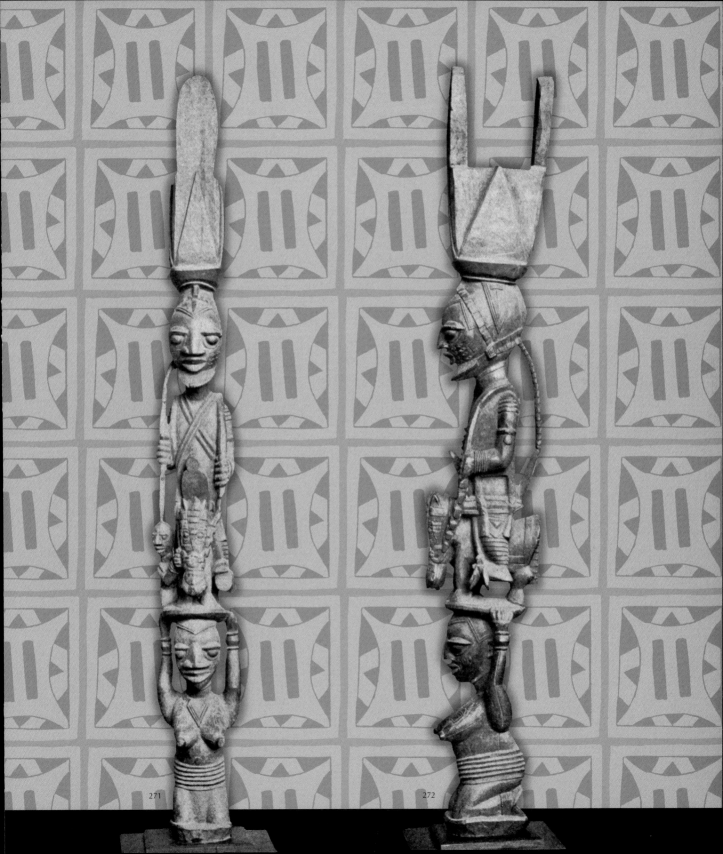

271   272

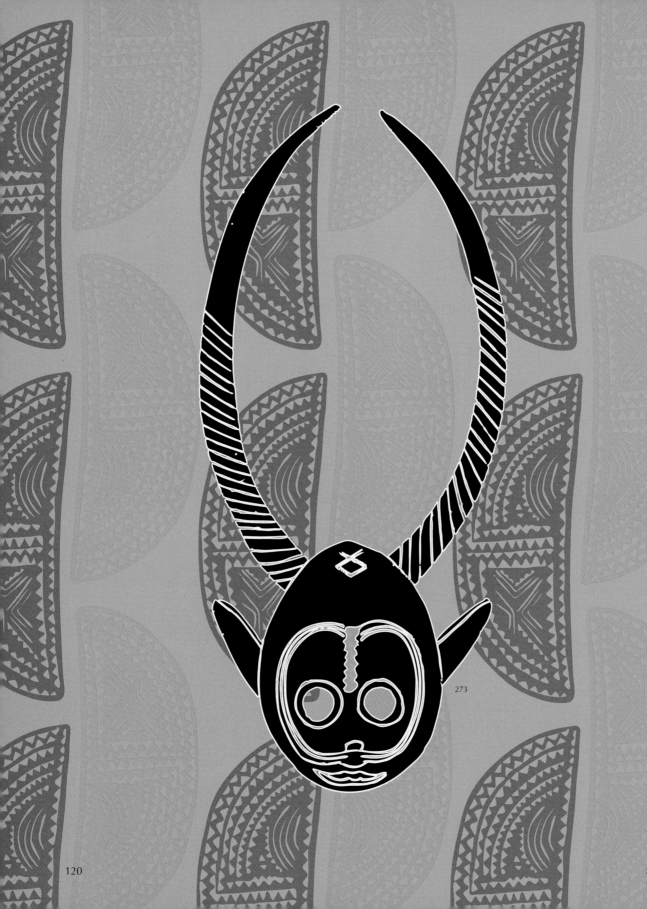

273

274 background

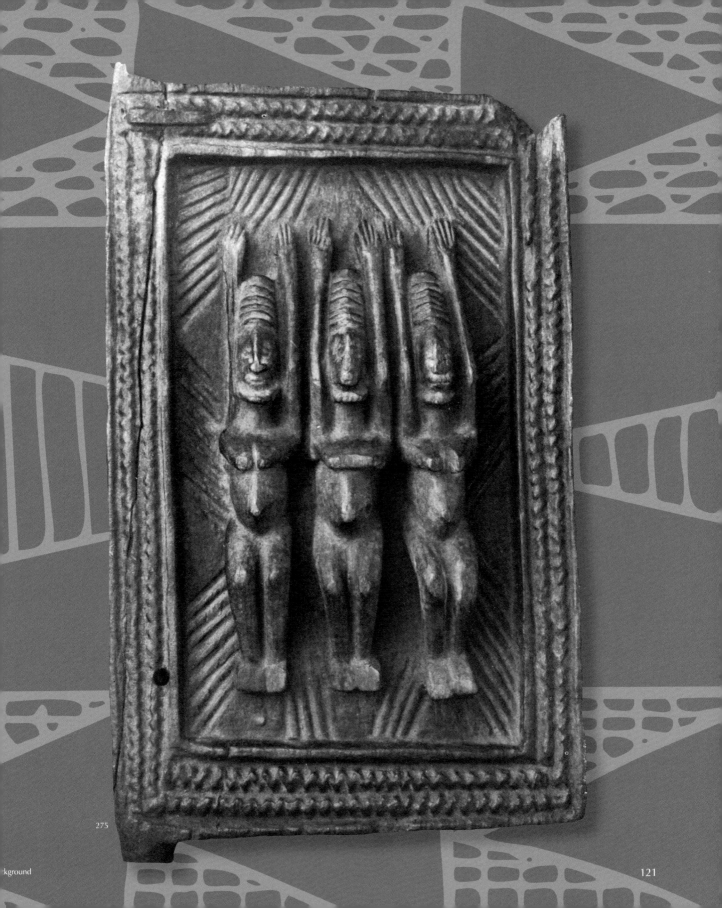

275

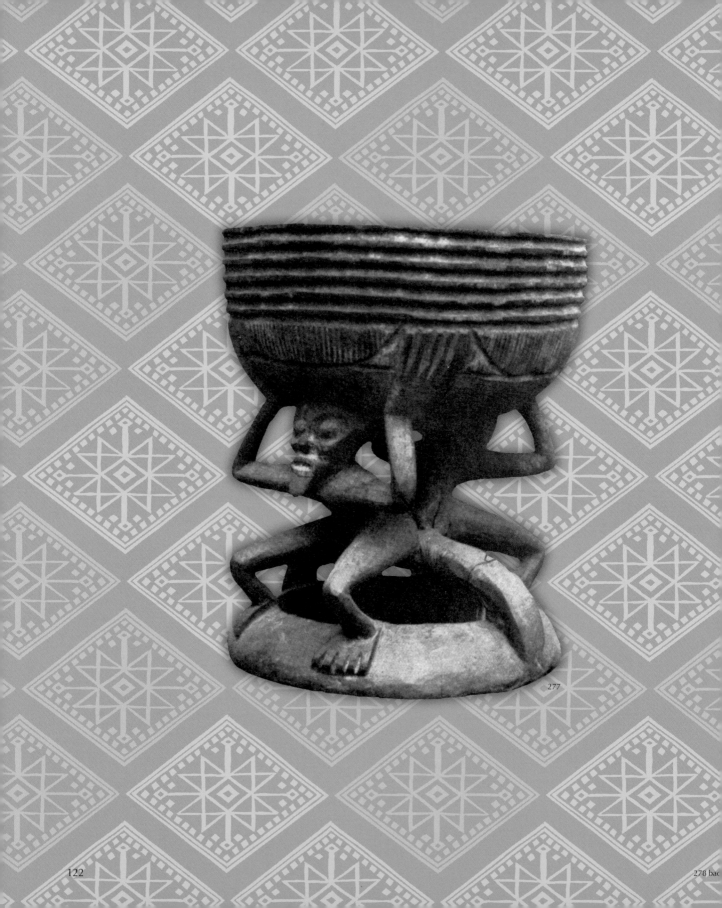

277

278 bac

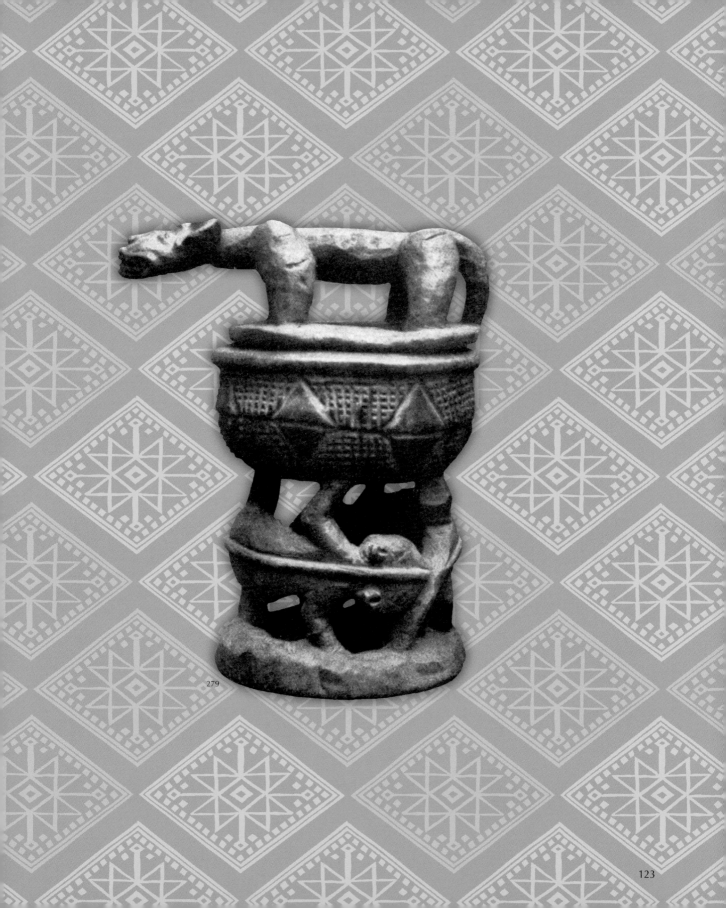

279

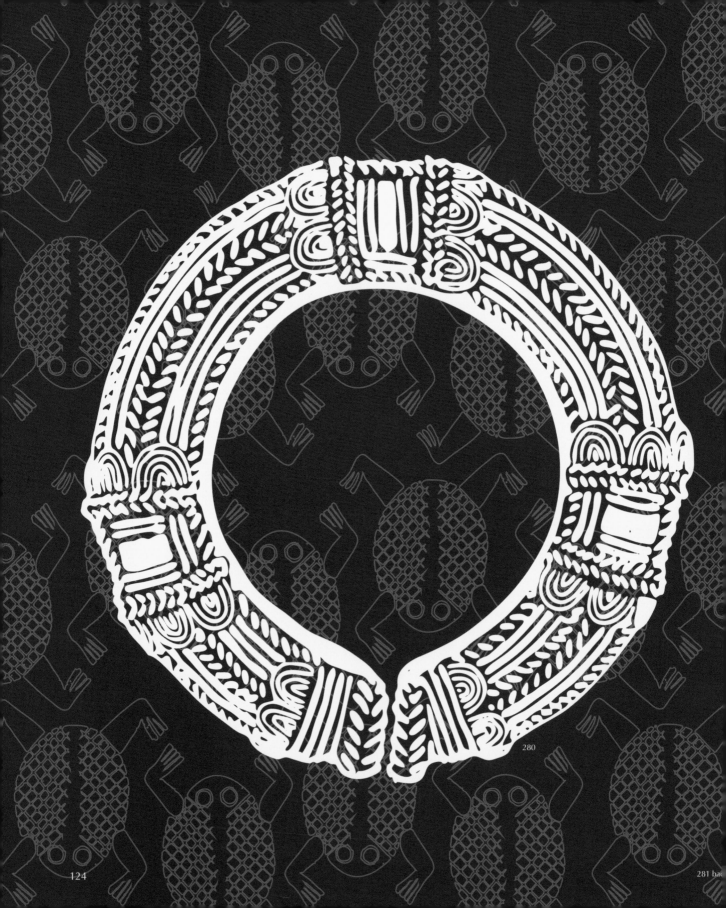

280

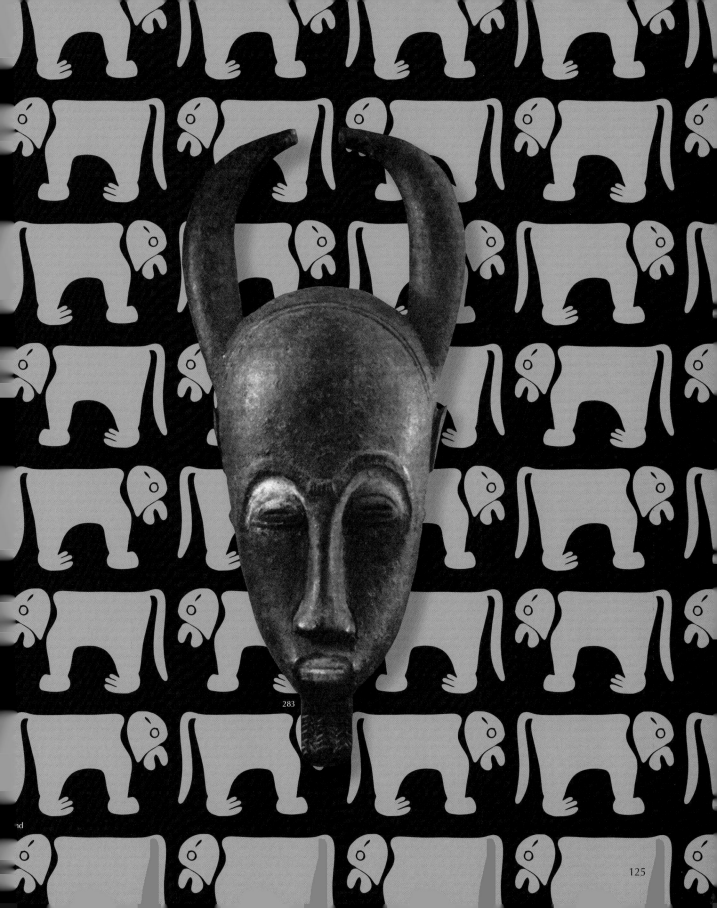

283

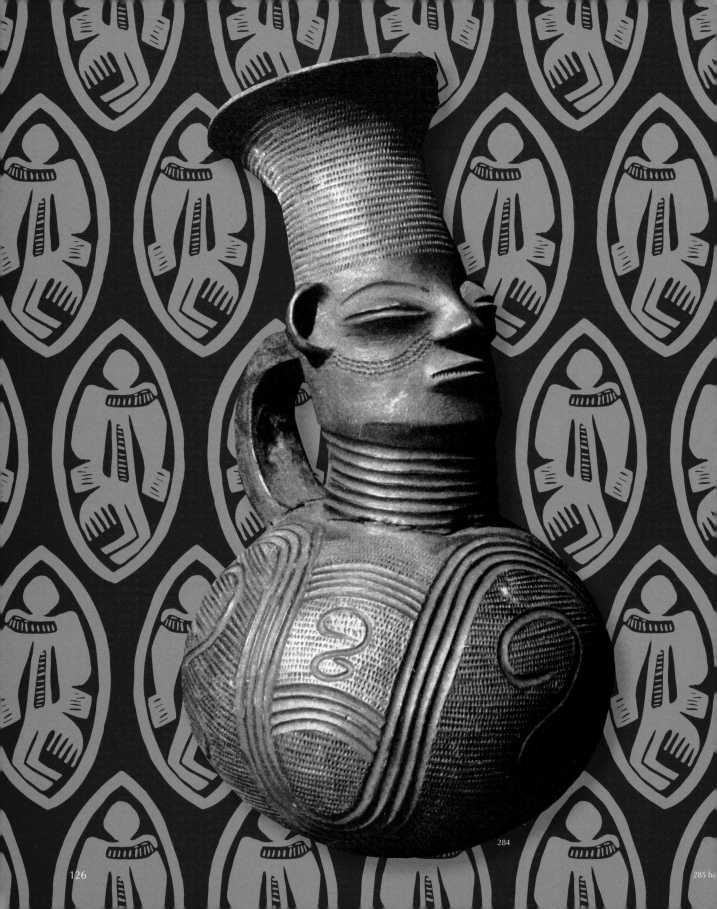

284

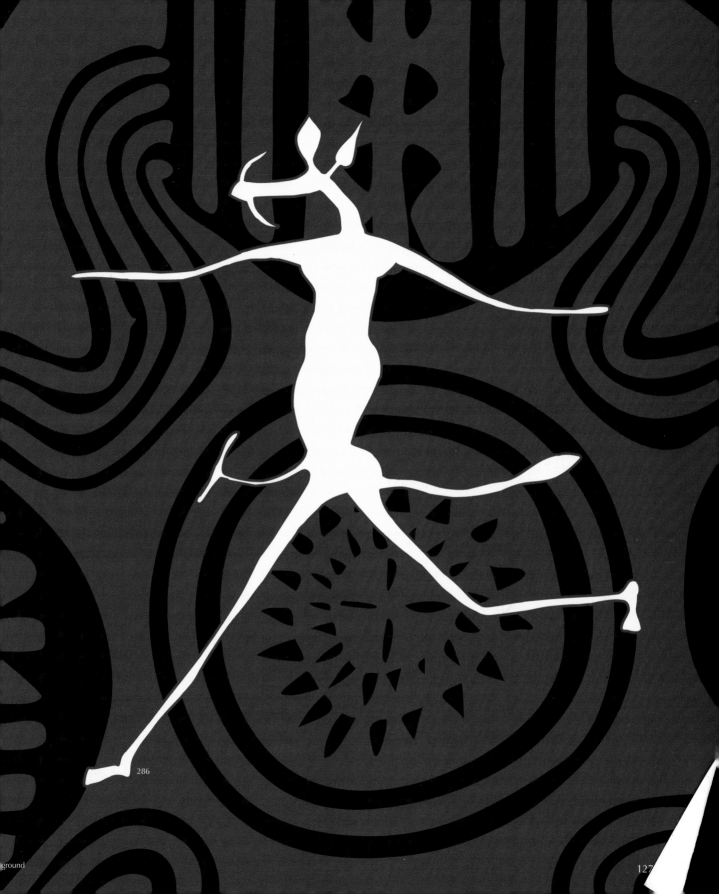

286

List of Vector Images

003	053	117	183	213	242	280
006	054	118	184	214	243	281
007	055	119	185	215	244	282
008	056	122	186	216	245	285
010	057	123	187	217	246	286
011	058	124	188	218	247	287
014	059	126	189	219	248	
016	060	131	190	220	249	
017	061	132	191	221	250	
021	063	133	193	222	251	
022	067	137	194	223	253	
023	068	138	195	224	254	
024	075	144	196	225	255	
025	076	145	197	226	256	
027	083	146	198	227	257	
029	084	151	199	228	258	
030	085	153	200	229	259	
031	090	159	201	230	261	
032	093	163	202	231	262	
035	097	164	203	232	263	
036	100	165	204	233	264	
037	101	169	205	234	265	
038	102	176	206	235	266	
039	103	177	207	236	268	
040	104	178	208	237	270	
042	105	179	209	238	273	
045	106	180	210	239	274	
046	109	181	211	240	276	
052	110	182	212	241	278	